嵩山少林寺武术馆武术教材

焦红波 主编

第一册

西北工业大学出版社

【内容简介】 本书主要包括少林武术的发展简史、少林武术的风格特点、少林武术的功能价值、少林基本功和基本技术、少林武术操、少林基本动作、少林小洪拳 24 式、少林通臂拳、少林朝阳拳、少林阴手棍等内容,对少林武术的传播发展,起到很大的促进作用。

适用于业界人士和少林武术研修者,可成为广大少林武术爱好者的良师善友、得力助手。

图书在版编目(CIP)数据

嵩山少林寺武术馆武术教材. 第一册 / 焦红波主编. —西安:西北工业大学出版社, 2016.12
 ISBN 978 - 7 - 5612 - 5169 - 0

Ⅰ. ①嵩… Ⅱ. ①焦… Ⅲ. ①少林武术—教材 Ⅳ. ①G852

中国版本图书馆 CIP 数据核字(2016)第 290422 号

出版发行:西北工业大学出版社
通信地址:西安市友谊西路 127 号　　邮编:710072
电　　话:(029)88493844　88491757
网　　址:www.nwpup.com
印　刷　者:陕西金德佳印务有限公司
开　　本:787 mm×1 092 mm　　1/16
印　　张:15.5
字　　数:277 千字
版　　次:2016 年 12 月第 1 版　2016 年 12 月第 1 次印刷
定　　价:48.00 元

编委会成员
Editorial Board Members

主 编：焦红波
Chief Editor：Jiao Hongbo

副主编：陈俊杰　　王松伟　　王占洋　　郑跃峰
Associate Editor：Chen Junjie　Wang Songwei
Wang Zhanyang　Zheng Yuefeng

执 笔：陈俊杰
Written by：Chen Junjie

编 委：
Editorial Board Members：

阎治军　　韩新强　　王占通　　焦晓伟
Yan Zhijun　　Han Xinqiang　　Wang Zhantong　　Jiao Xiaowei
焦宏敏　　蒋东旭　　吕宏军　　李振亮
Jiao Hongmin　　Jiang Dongxu　　Lü Hongjun　　Li Zhenliang
景冠飞　　刘珊珊　　吴卫永　　董 伟
Jing Guanfei　　Liu Shanshan　　Wu Weiyong　　Dong Wei

翻 译：李广升　　陈中纪
Translator：Li Guangsheng　Chen Zhongji

嵩山少林寺
武术馆武术教材

徐才
乙酉年秋

展武艺雄姿

扬中华国威

李佑生

宏揚中華瑰寶振
興民族精神

贈少林寺武術館

宋任窮戊辰夏日

贺少林寺武术馆开馆

名山名刹名拳
国威国宝国魂

杨成武
一九八八年九月

少林武术
前程锦绣

李梦华

序

寇武江[1]

  缘于工作我与同事一起到嵩山少林寺武术馆调研,在观看队员表演练功后,红波告诉我,武术馆拟出版一本少林武术教材,并希望我能为之作序。说实话,近段时间对于武术文化与旅游的研究,我虽然下了一点功夫,但对少林武术的套路招式技法学习我可是一窍不通。然而,考虑到出版教材,传承文化,规范练习,是件功在当今、利在后人的好事,我便答应了。

  少林武术在河南旅游文化品牌中极具代表性,在国内外享有盛名。自北魏以来,少林武术伴随着少林寺禅宗的发展,历经1 500多年的沧桑岁月,积淀了丰富而深厚的文化内涵。20世纪80年代,国家旅游局和河南省人民政府共同投资兴建少林寺武术馆时,就依托少林寺"拳以寺名,寺以武显"的文化内涵,将演武厅列入中原旅游区重点工程项目进行建设。其目的是宣传弘扬深厚的河南文化,满足广大武术爱好者和游客学习少林武术和观看少林武术表演的要求。武术馆自1988年开馆至今,以少林武术这一独特的旅游文化为基础,积极开展少林武术国际文化交流和武术教学研究活动,推动了少林武术专项游,吸引了国内外成千上万的武术爱好者前来参观、学习少林武术,培养出了一大批高层次的少林武术专业人才,为宣传弘扬少林武术文化,促进河南旅游业可持续发展做出了突出贡献。

  少林寺在历史上屡遭兵燹,几经兴衰,少林武术也屡遭摧残,濒临失传。20世纪80年代,国家对传统武术文化给予了高度重视,对长期保存于少林高僧及民间武术名师中的珍贵少林武术资料进行了挖掘收集整理,以不同的方式予以出版发行,对少林武术的传播发展起到很大的促进作用,但以教材的形式出版的则很少。

  少林寺武术馆集聚着众多少林武术名家及武坛精英,他们在工作之余

---

[1] 寇武江:河南省旅游局局长。

长期致力于少林武术文化的研究,并把研究成果在实践中加以验证,不断地修正传统套路中技法理论及技法运用。本书就是他们对少林武术文化研究的成果和近30年来长期从事表演、教学、交流工作经验的积累结晶。我相信本书出版以后,一定会给业界人士和广大少林武术研修者提供一个好的参考,成为广大少林武术爱好者的良师善友、得力助手。

是为序。

2015年6月5日

Preface

By Kou Wujiang[①]

  Due to a work visit to the Shaolin Temple Wushu Training Center with my colleagues, Hongbo asked me after I watched their kungfu performance and training to provide a preface to the textbook that they were preparing to publish about Shaolin martial arts. Frankly speaking, I know little about martial arts forms and combat techniques, although I did spend some time researching martial arts culture and tourism. However, considering that the textbook would bring significant benefits not only for Shaolin cultural heritage but also for students of martial arts, I said yes.

  Shaolin Martial Arts is a recognized brand for Henan cultural tourism and it enjoys a great reputation around the world. Since the Northern Wei Dynasty, Shaolin martial arts, along with Shaolin Zen culture, has been developed for more than 1,500 years. A rich and profound cultural tradition was nurtured and cultivated during this period. During the 80's of the last century, the China National Tourism Administration and the People's Government of Henan province built the Shaolin Temple Wushu Training Center based on a cultural philosophy of the Shaolin Temple, "The martial arts are recognized by the fame of the Shaolin Temple and the Temple is recognized by martial arts." The Shaolin Wushu Training Center was envisioned to play a key role in China's central region tourism project for spreading Henan's culture and meeting the peoples' desire to practice Shaolin Kungfu and watch Kungfu performances. Since 1988, the Wushu Center has carried out international communications and undertaken teaching activities based upon martial arts. Millions of tourists have been

---

① Kou Wujiang: Director General of Henan Provincial Tourism Administration.

attracted to visit the center and experience martial arts through specialized Shaolin tourism. Moreover, a large number of high level martial arts masters have been trained here. The center has made great contributions to the promotion of Shaolin martial arts as well as Henan's sustainable tourism development.

The Shaolin Temple has seen destruction several times in its history and Shaolin martial arts has also encountered challenges, even to the point of almost suffering extinction. In the 80's of the last century, our nation paid great attention to traditional martial arts culture, to systematically excavate and preserve the martial arts materials derived from prominent Shaolin monks and folk Kungfu masters. The materials were published through different methods to develop and promote Shaolin martial arts more effectively. However, published textbooks with an emphasis on teaching are rarely seen.

The Shaolin Temple Wushu Training Center has gathered many Shaolin Wushu masters and professionals who have devoted themselves in the long run to Shaolin martial arts culture research as well as to ensure that the research results can be put into practice; as well as continuous efforts of revising the technical theories and applications in the traditional practice sets. This textbook is the product of the accumulation of their research results in Shaolin wushu culture and the working experience through their performance, teaching and exchange over two decades. I believe that after this texbook is published, it will serve as an excellent reference to the people in the industry and to the general public who are interested in practicing Shaolin wushu.

The above serves as a foreword.

June 05, 2015

前　言

焦红波[①]

　　少林武术是中国宝贵的文化遗产,是武林中的一颗璀璨明珠。它内容广博,种类繁多,技法精湛,享誉中外。习练少林武术,不仅可以强健筋骨,防身抗暴,还可以陶冶情操,祛病延年。少林武术内静外猛、朴实无华、刚柔相济、立足实战,现已发展成为海内外广为流传的健身运动之一。

　　少林武术因发源于嵩山少林寺而得名。千百年来,作为少林武术发祥地的少林寺,因闻名天下的少林功夫和禅宗祖庭而被誉为"天下第一名刹"。地处少林寺的登封,因少林武术运动开展得非常广泛,也被称为"武术之乡"。为了传承与弘扬博大精深的少林武术,使少林武术以更大的步伐走向世界,1988年,作为向海内外传授少林武术基地的嵩山少林寺武术馆在少林武术发祥地诞生了。

　　河南省嵩山少林寺武术馆自创办之后,中外少林武术爱好者闻讯而至,习武练功。到目前为止,嵩山少林寺武术馆已培养了世界100多个国家和地区的武术学员2万余人。武馆自建立以来还为数以千万计的中外来宾展示精湛的少林武术。同时,嵩山少林寺武术馆还应邀到世界80多个国家和地区传授少林武术,使之在世界上生根、开花、结果。

　　嵩山少林寺武术馆由于地处少林武术发祥地和武术之乡的优势,汇集了众多少林武术高手在此传武研武,可谓人才济济。自建馆起,武术馆在传授少林武术的同时,还不断对少林武术进行深入的研究、挖掘和整理,并编写了许多具有代表性的少林武术文化书籍,为少林武术的传播和光大起到了重要的作用。

　　当前,在传习少林武术的过程中,系统、规范的少林武术教材的缺失致使少林武术在传播过程中出现诸多对其曲解和误解的现象。嵩山少林寺武

---

① 焦红波:河南省嵩山少林寺武术馆馆长、总教练,本书主编。

术馆作为国家建立的传播、弘扬和研究少林武术的中心,有责任、有义务编写一部权威性的介绍少林武术的书籍,以便为人们系统和完整学习少林武术提供强有力的保障。

本次编写的少林武术教材内容分为少林武术概论、少林武术基本动作和少林武术基本套路三部分。全书系统论述和介绍了少林武术的理论和具体习练方法,是学习和研究少林武术的必备之教材。本书按照少林武术一至九段的评位要求,分初级、中级、高级三个阶段,选取了少林十八势、少林烧火棍、少林长拳、七星拳、八段锦、易筋经等作为练习的功法,从而为求取段位者顺利通过段位的考核提供最有效的途径。特别要提出的是,本书中的部分内容,是我们与国家体委武术挖掘小组和北京体育大学门惠丰教授于20世纪80年代初共同创编的,经过多年的教学实践反映良好。

少林武术历史悠久,技法精湛,内容博大,需要探索和研究的还很多。因而在编写少林武术书籍之时,编写人员虽竭尽全力,但书中不当之处也再所难免,敬希各位方家及广大武术爱好者不吝赐教,以使其日臻完善。

2016年8月20日

Foreword

By Jiao Hongbo[1]

Shaolin martial arts is a bright pearl and the precious cultural heritage of China. It enjoys enormous popularity throughout the world for its broad content, variety of types and exquisite techniques. Practicing martial arts can not only strengthen the muscles and bones, but also cultivate sentiments and keep healthy. Now it has become a popular worldwide sport due to its graceful and powerful movements, internal static, external fierce and actual combat experiences.

Shaolin martial arts originated from the Shaolin Temple, hence the name. It was reputed as the "No. 1 Temple under Heaven". Dengfeng city, where the Shaolin Temple was located, was renowned as the "Hometown of Chinese Kungfu" for the popular participation. In 1988, the Shaolin Temple Wushu Training Center was founded in Shaolin Village, its purpose is to inherit and carry forward the extensive and profound Shaolin martial arts.

Numerous enthusiasts of Shaolin Kungfu both in China and abroad practiced here, up to now, more than 20,000 students from over 100 countries and regions have been trained in this center. Tens of millions of visitors have enjoyed the consummate Kungfu shows since the establishment of the Wushu Training Center. Meanwhile professional coaches from this center have been invited to visit over 80 countries and regions to teach and impart Shaolin skills.

The Shaolin Temple Wushu Training Center is just located in the birthplace of Shaolin martial arts and the "Hometown of Chinese Kungfu", so numerous

---

[1] Jiao Hongbo: Director, Chief Coach of Shaolin Temple Wushu Training Center, Mt. Songshan, Henan Province.

Kungfu masters gathered in this Training Center to study and practice. After couple of years of in-depth research, exploration and collecting, the Training Center composed a number of representative books which played an important role in promotion and popularity of Shaolin martial arts.

Systematic, standard and practical textbook is needed in order to avoid the phenomenon of misunderstanding and misinterpreting the discipline of Kungfu practices. As the state-level teaching base, the Shaolin Temple Wushu Training Center has the responsibility to compile this authoritative book to provide standard practices.

This Shaolin martial arts textbook consists of three parts: Introduction to Shaolin Martial Arts, Basic Shaolin Boxing Routines, and Basic Skills and Movements of Shaolin Martial Arts. The book, indispensable for studying Shaolin martial arts, describes systematically the theory and methods of Shaolin martial arts. Based on the requirements of Chinese martial arts Duan Ranking System from 1 to 9, the book describes selected Shaolin 18 Forms, Shaolin Shaohuo Stick, Shaolin Long Boxing, Shaolin Seven-star Boxing, Eight-sectioned Exercise(Baduanjin) and Channel-changing Scriptures(Yijinjing) as primary, middle and higher Dan(Rank) practicing routines, to make people who want to get higher grading in the examination have efficient way. It is necessary to be pointed out additionally that some parts of the textbook were completed with the cooperation of the martial arts research and exploration group of National Sports Commission and Professor Men Huifeng of Beijing Sports University in the early 1980s. The parts had produced notable effect by over years teaching practice.

Shaolin martial arts has a long history, consummate techniques, rich content which must be continually explored and studied. We have tried our best to finish this book, but we are still afraid there are some places that need to be perfected, so comments and suggestions will be greatly appreciated.

August 20th, 2016

目 录
CONTENT

第一章　少林武术概论

Chapter 1　Introduction to Shaolin Martial Arts ………… 1

　　第一节　少林武术的发展简史

　　Quarter 1　Origin and Development of Shaolin Martial Arts ………… 1

　　第二节　少林武术的风格特点

　　Quarter 2　Content and Style Features of Shaolin Maritial Arts ………… 6

　　第三节　少林武术的功能价值

　　Quarter 3　Fitness Effect of Shaolin Maritial Arts ………… 10

第二章　少林基本功和基本技术

Chapter 2　Shaolin Basic Arts and Basic Techniques ………… 12

　　第一节　少林桩功(少林基本功法)

　　Quarter 1　Shaolin Piling(Shaolin Basic Arts) ………… 12

　　第二节　少林基本技术

　　Quarter 2　Shaolin Basic Techniques ………… 16

第三章　少林武术操

Chapter 3　Shaolin Martial Arts Exercise ………… 39

　　第一节　套路动作名称

　　Quarter 1　Routine Names ………… 39

　　第二节　套路动作图解

　　Quarter 2　Figures of Routine Movements ………… 39

第四章　少林基本动作(少林十八势)

Chapter 4　Shaolin Basic Movements（Shaolin 18 Forms） ………… 65

　　第一节　套路动作名称

Quarter 1　Routine Names ………………………………… 65
第二节　套路动作图解
Quarter 2　Figures of Routine Movements ……………………………… 66

第五章　少林小洪拳 24 式
Chapter 5　Shaolin Xiaohong Boxing（24 Forms）……………… 108
第一节　套路名称
Quarter 1　Routine Names ………………………………… 108
第二节　套路动作图解
Quarter 2　Figures of Routine Movements ……………………………… 109

第六章　少林通背拳
Chapter 6　Shaolin Tongbei Boxing ………………………… 132
第一节　套路动作名称
Quarter 1　Routine Names ………………………………… 132
第二节　套路动作图解
Quarter 2　Figures of Routine Movements ……………………………… 133

第七章　少林朝阳拳
Chapter 7　Shaolin Chaoyang Boxing ……………………… 160
第一节　套路动作名称
Quarter 1　Routine Names ………………………………… 160
第二节　套路动作图解
Quarter 2　Figures of Routine Movements ……………………………… 161

第八章　少林阴手棍
Chapter 8　Shaolin Yinshou Stick …………………………… 192
第一节　套路动作名称
Quarter 1　Routine Names ………………………………… 192
第二节　套路动作图解
Quarter 2　Figures of Routine Movements ……………………………… 193

第一章　少林武术概论

Chapter 1　Introduction to Shaolin Martial Arts

第一节　少林武术的发展简史

Quarter 1　Origin and Development of Shaolin Martial Arts

少林武术源于少林寺，拳因寺而得名，故称少林拳。少林寺位于河南省登封市城西北约13千米处，该寺系北魏孝文帝太和十九年（495年）为印度僧人跋陀来中国传播佛教所建造。由于寺院建立在少室山阴的密林中，故称少林寺。

Originated from Shaolin Temple, Shaolin Martial Arts hence named. Lying about 13 kilometers northwest of Dengfeng City, Henan Province, Shaolin Temple was established in the 19th year of Taihe of Emperor Xiaowen of the Northern Wei Dynasty (495) for Indian Monk Batuo to spread Buddhism in China. Since the temple was established in dense woods at the foot of Shaoshi Mountains, hence the name.

少林寺的建成，吸引了四方众多的佛教信徒，北魏孝明帝孝昌三年（527年）印度僧人菩提达摩来中国河南嵩山少林寺传授佛教禅宗。他不主张用文字传教，而采用"壁观"的办法，静坐修心。众僧每日坐禅参悟，时间一长必然气血不和，精神疲倦，日渐疲弱，直接影响众僧坐禅和传教。寺院又在深山之中，人烟稀少，猛兽出没无常，直接威胁着众僧的生命。"人，飞不如禽，走不如兽，禽兽以爪牙扑人，人以智技制服禽兽。"这就使众僧开始寻求健体强身技击之法，当时一位名叫僧稠的和尚，体格健壮，"抱肩筑腰，气嘘顶上"（唐·道宣《续高僧传》）能"引重千钧，其拳捷骁劲"（唐·张鷟《朝野佥载》），可算是少林寺最早的武僧。

Shaolin Temple attracted numerous Buddhists from far and near. In the 3rd year of Xiaochang of Emperor Xiaoming of the Northern Wei Dynasty (527), Indian Monk Bodhidharma came to Shaolin Temple to preach Zen Buddhism. He focused on meditation instead of preaching with texts. Long-term meditation caused disharmony of vital energy and blood, mental fatigue and vulnerability. In the sparsely populated mountains, wild beasts often appeared, directly threatening the monks. "Human beings can not match birds in terms of flying, or beasts in term of running. Beasts attack human beings with claws and teeth, human beings should beat beasts with wisdom." This made the monks seek physical fitness and martial arts. Seng Chou can be regarded as the first Shaolin Temple warrior monk. He was "strong as a horse, characterized by sturdy frame" (Monk Shih Dao Hsuan · the Tang Dynasty *Continuation of Biographies of Eminent Monks*), and "brave and good at fighting" (Zhang Wu · the Tang Dynasty *Selected Records of the Court and the Commonalty*).

少林拳的形成和发展,实际上是历代众僧参照我国民间长期流传的健身技击术,以及他家拳术之特长,兼收并蓄,融汇贯通,长期演练的结果。特别是在隋末唐初,少林寺已发展成一个拥有百顷田产的大佛寺。隋末全国各地爆发了农民起义,加上唐高祖武德四年(621年),秦王李世民与在洛阳的王世充交战,在战争的关紧时刻,少林寺僧以昙宗、志操、惠扬等为首出兵相助,击溃郑军,活捉了王世充的侄子王仁则。少林寺僧的这一行动,有力地支援了唐军,沉重打击了郑军,加速了王世充的灭亡。为表彰少林众僧助战有功,李世民登基后,给少林寺以嘉奖。唐郑之战给少林寺武僧以显武的机会,大唐皇帝的颁奖宣慰和封赐也使少林寺从此声名日隆,寺院发展很快,名僧层出不穷。习武性质较此前大不相同,习武扬名,习武立功受封,强烈地刺激着少林寺僧的习武热情,将习武与实践紧密地联系在一起,少林和尚实际变成了皇家所供养的一只特殊军队。从此众僧习武之风成为少林寺世代相传的独特宗风。

Shaolin Boxing formation and development were based on long-term folk martial arts and expertise. By the late Sui and early Tang dynasties, Shaolin Temple had developed into a large Buddhist temple with several thousand hectares of property estate. In the 4th year of Wude of Emperor Gaozu of the Tang Dynasty (621), Prince Qin Li Shimin and Warlord Wang Shichong in Luoyang were at war. Shaolin warrior monks, led by Tan Zong, Zhi Cao and Hui Yang, helped Prince Qin Li Shimin and defeated Warlord Wang Shichong, capturing his nephew Wang Renze. Li Shimin, Emperor Taizong of the Tang Dynasty, commended Shaolin monks after he ascended the throne, making Shaolin Temple increasingly famous and popular and witness numerous famous monks. Martial arts practicing became based on fame and merits, strongly stimulating Shaolin monk martial arts practicing enthusiasm and combining martial arts practicing with the society. Shaolin monks actually became a special army dependent on the imperial court. Since then martial arts practicing has been a unique elegance of Shaolin monks passing on from generation to generation.

宋代少林寺发展兴旺、规模宏大,僧众达两千多人,方丈福居大和尚,为发展少林武术,曾邀请全国十八家武林高手会武于少林寺,进行武功技法交流。广泛吸取众家之长,最后汇集成册,供寺僧学习演练。清《拳经》云,宋朝开国皇帝赵匡胤亦精于少林拳,还传有少林太祖长拳。宋代既然有僧兵,说明宋代寺僧习武是可以肯定的。

In the Song Dynasty, Shaolin Temple boomed, hosting over 2,000 monks. For the development of Shaolin Martial Arts, Abbot Fuju invited top martial artists from 18 schools to Shaolin Temple to exchange martial arts techniques which were extensively selected and integrated into a book. According to *Classic Boxing* of the Qing Dynasty, Zhao Kuangyin, founding emperor of the Song Dynasty mastered Shaolin Boxing and created Shaolin Taizu Long Boxing. Warrior Monks in the Song Dynasty highlight martial arts practicing then.

元朝,少林寺僧习武之风不减。据《少林寺志》记载:元至正年间,日本僧人邵元和尚长期居住少林寺,他精通汉文,擅长书法,初任书记,后任首座僧,并得到少林武僧之传授,后来回国后,将少林武术带到日本,广为传播,深受日本人民的尊敬和喜爱,被日本国民称之为"国魂"。

In the Yuan Dynasty, Shaolin monks kept martial arts practicing. According to *Shaolin Temple Chronicles*, in the years of Zhizheng of the Yuan Dynasty, Japanese Monk Shao Yuan stayed in Shaolin Temple permanently. Fluent in Chinese and good at calligraphy, he was made a clerk monk at first and a chief monk later. Taught by Shaolin warrior monks, he brought Shaolin Martial Arts to Japan, widely disseminated and well received by the Japanese people, and known as "national soul".

明代是中华武术全面发展的重要历史时期,民间武术争奇斗艳,各放异彩。少林武术在这一时期达到巅峰,誉满天下。

The Ming Dynasty witnessed comprehensive development of Chinese martial arts, different civil martial arts contesting and growing. Shaolin Martial Arts reached its peak.

抗倭名将戚继光《纪效新书·拳经提要篇》云:"少林棍……皆今之有名者。"明著名武术家茅元仪在《武备志》中写道:"诸艺宗于棍,棍宗于少林。"据历史资料记载:明代少林寺僧习武人数最多,月空、小山等和尚痛击倭寇,屡立战功,表现了少林寺僧武艺高强、英勇杀敌的爱国精神。明朝从洪武到崇祯的260多年间,武僧多至万余人,其中应诏为将者和武林高手达数百余人。总之,明代是少林武术发展的极盛时期。

New Book Recording Effective Techniques · Classic Boxing Abstract by Qi Jiguang, a famous general of the Ming Dynasty, reads, "there are well-known Shaolin Stick practitioners such as …". *Records of Military Preparations* by famous martial artist Mao Yuanyi of the Ming Dynasty reads, "Various arts originated from stick, and stick originated from Shaolin". According to historical records, the Ming Dynasty witnessed the largest number of Shaolin martial arts practicing monks, such as Yuekong and Xiaoshan who fought against Japanese pirates and made military exploits. The 260-year period from Hongwu to Chongzhen witnessed over 10,000 warrior monks, including several hundred monk generals and top martial artists. In short, the Ming Dynasty was the most flourishing period of Shaolin Martial Arts.

清代,雍正时期,清政府严禁教武练武,少林寺习武之风曾一度遭禁,练武活动由公开转入暗地练武。少林寺众僧继承和恪守禅武一体的宗风,把昼习经、夜练武作为自己修行的最重要的两件事。今少林寺西方圣人殿内,青砖地面上仍留存有当时寺僧练功所形成的48个凹陷脚窝,殿内还存有兵器架等物,显然,这是少林寺僧长期从事武功训练的专门殿堂。清末,少林寺日趋衰败,一片破落景象,少林寺僧纷纷出走,星散各地,成了游方僧人。清政府禁止习武,不仅没有灭绝少林武功,反而把少林武术推向了民间,对少林武术的广泛传播起到了推动作用。

In the period under the reign of Emperor Yongzheng of the Qing Dynasty, practicing of martial arts including Shaolin Martial Arts was prohibited. Practicing of martial arts was conducted secretly. Abiding by integration of practicing of martial arts and meditation, Shaolin monks meditated by day and practiced martial arts at night. Today, in the Western Sage Hall of Shaolin Temple, there are 48 footprint depressions formed by martial arts practicing and weapon racks, indicating it used to be a martial arts training hall. In the late Qing Dynasty, Shaolin Temple declined. Many monks left, wandering all over the country. The Qing government banned martial arts practicing, which only promoted Shaolin Martial Arts to the community instead of eliminating it.

民国年间,寺院僧人逐渐减少,当时政府虽然没有禁止习武,但也无济于助,而在寺院的寺僧们依然苦行习武。1928年,军阀混战,石友三与樊钟秀战于河南,樊设司令部于少林寺,石友三攻占少林寺后,火焚少林寺,大火漫燃40余天,殿堂楼阁等古建筑被夷为平地,大量珍贵文物遭到破坏。

In the period of the Republic of China, the number of monks gradually decreased. The government then did not ban martial arts practicing or promote it. The monks continued martial arts practicing. In 1928, Warlords Shi Yousan and Fan Zhongxiu fought in Henan. The latter was headquartered in Shaolin Temple and the former burnt Shaolin Temple after he captured it. The fire lasted more than 40 days, burning down some of the ancient buildings and destroyed numerous historic relics.

新中国成立后,少林寺和少林武术又获得了新生。政府拨专款修复了少林寺。特别是香港中原影业公司以少林武术为原素材摄制的功夫片《少林寺》轰动了国内外,久负盛名的少林武术倾倒了无数观众。国内外武术爱好者、慕名来少林寺投师习武者络绎不绝。1988年国家投资兴建了宏伟壮观的"远东国际武术培训中心"——河南省嵩山少林寺武术馆。武术馆的落成标志着少林武术进入了一个崭新的时代,是我国第一所面向海内外招生、培养武术专业人才、传播少林武术,集武术、旅游、接待为一体的综合性涉外武术培训基地。由武艺高超的少林武僧和俗家弟子亲自传授功夫,师资力量雄厚、教学设施齐全、环境条件优越、有现代化表演厅、练功房、室外演武场,堪称我国一流武术训练和武术旅游中心。

After the founding of new China, Shaolin Temple and Shaolin Martial Arts gained a new life. The state allocated funds to repair Shaolin Temple. The martial arts film *Shaolin Temple* produced by Chung Yuen Motion Picture Co. with Shaolin Martial Arts as the original footage created a sensation at home and abroad. The prestigious Shaolin Martial Arts attracted countless viewers. Martial arts enthusiasts at home and abroad came to Shaolin Temple for martial arts practicing. In 1988, the state built "Far East International Martial Arts Training

Center"—Henan Songshan Shaolin Temple Wushu Training Center, marking a new era of Shaolin Martial Arts. This center is China's first integrated international martial arts training center merging domestic and international recruitment, martial artists training, Shaolin Martial Arts promotion, martial arts, tourism and hospitality into a single whole. As China's first-class martial arts training and martial arts tourism center, it is characterized by strong faculty, complete facilities, excellent environment, modern performance halls, martial arts practicing rooms, and outdoor martial arts practicing fields.

少林寺武术馆主要承担国际、国内武术交流、教学和表演任务。建馆近30年来，先后应邀到亚、欧、美、澳、非等五大洲的80多个国家和地区进行过上千场表演，观众千万余人。先后接待了数十万世界各地的武术爱好者来研修功夫和归宗朝圣，是中华大地上的一颗璀璨明珠。

This center focuses on domestic and international martial arts exchanges, teaching and performances. Over the last 2 decades, it has conducted over 1,000performances with nearly 10 million viewers in over 60 countries and regions in Asia, Europe, America, Oceania and Africa, received several hundred thousand martial arts enthusiasts around the world for martial arts practicing and pilgrimage.

第二节　少林武术的风格特点
Quarter 2　Content and Style Features of Shaolin Maritial Arts

一、内容

少林武术内容丰富，特点突出，体系完整，既有拳术套路，又有器械套路；既有技击散打、对练，又有气功和功法修练。

Section 1　Content

Shaolin Boxing has rich content, prominent features, and complete system, covering Chinese boxing routines, weapon routines, free combat, sparring, and vital energy and arts practicing.

拳术：少林拳单练，既有刚劲突出的外功拳，也有柔和无比的内功拳。

第一章 少林武术概论

外功拳有小洪拳、大洪拳、老洪拳、朝阳拳、长拳、梅花拳、炮拳、罗汉拳、通背（臂）拳、长护心意门拳、七星拳、关东拳以及青龙出海拳、护身流星拳、金刚拳等；内功拳有心意拳和柔拳；对练拳术有扳手六合、咬手六合、耳把六合、踢打六合等。

Chinese boxing: Shaolin Boxing soloing, covering bold and prominent coming force boxing and soft inner power boxing. Coming force boxing includes Small-form Hong Boxing, Big-form Hong Boxing, Original Hong Boxing, Zhaoyang Boxing, Long Boxing, Plum Boxing, Cannon Boxing, Arhat Boxing, Back-pressing Boxing, Protective Mind-and-will Boxing, Seven-star Boxing, Guandong Boxing and Chang-style Boxing, Protective Meteor Boxing and Warrior Boxing. Inner power boxing includes Mind-and-will Boxing and Soft Boxing. Sparring Chinese boxing includes Wrestling Six-Harmony, Gripping Six-Harmony, Slapping Six-Harmony and Kicking Six-Harmony.

器械：少林拳的器械分单练和对练，单练器械有梅花刀、开山刀、老单刀、达磨剑、乾坤剑、龙行剑、少林烧火棍、眉齐棍、猿猴棍、镇山棍、双盘龙棍、梢子棍、二十一名枪、四十八名枪、六合枪、十三枪、杨家枪、朴刀、春秋大刀、方便铲、三股叉、劈四门震刀、滚堂双刀、双草镰、双拐等；对练器械有白手夺枪、白手夺刀、双枪对刺、刀破刀、大刀破枪、朴刀破枪、单刀破枪、双刀破枪、匕首破枪、单拐破枪、棍破枪、梢子棍破枪、六合棍、三节棍破枪等。

Weapons: Shaolin Boxing weapons consist of soloing and sparring. Soloing weapons include plum broadsword, quarrying broadsword, short-hilted broadsword, Dharma Sword, Qiankun Sword, Longxing Sword, Shaolin Shaohuo Stick, Eyebrow Stick, Monkey Stick, Zhengshan Stick, Shuangpanlong Stick, Mortise Pin Stick, 21-spear, 48-spear, Six-Harmony Spear, 13-spear, Yang Style Spear, Long-handled Broadsword, Spring and Autumn Broadsword, Convenience Spade, Three-tined Fork, Array-breaking Broadsword, Rolling Double Broadswords, Double Sickles and Double Crutches. Sparring weapons include Bare-handed vs. Spear, Bare-handed vs. Broadsword, Spear vs. Spear, Broadsword vs. Broadsword, Broadsword vs. Spear, Long-handled Broadsword vs. Spear, Single Broadsword vs. Spear, Double Broadswords vs. Spear, Dagger vs. Spear, Single Crutch vs. Spear, Stick vs. Spear, Mortise Pin Stick vs. Spear, Six-Harmony Stick, and Three-section Stick vs Spear.

技击和散打：有闪战移身把、虎刺把、心意把、游龙飞步、丹凤朝阳、近身靠打、拔步炮、小鬼篡枪、鹞子钻林等百余种。功法修炼：有易筋经、洗髓经、神勇八段锦、小武功、混元一气排打功、阴阳气功、硬气功等。

Free combat: more than 100 forms such as Lightning Moving, Tiger Assassinating Form, Mind-and-will Moving Form, Swift Moving, Flying Phoenix, Close Quarters Combat, Striding Cannon, Spear Seizing and Kite Flying in Forest. Arts: Channel-changing Scriptures, Marrow Washing Scriptures, Brave Eight Movements, Little Martial Arts, Over-all Vital Energy Brick, Yin-Yang Vital Energy and Hard Vital Energy.

二、风格与特点

少林拳之所以能够千年流传，受人敬仰，主要是因为功夫过硬，风格独特，立足于实战。

Section 2　Style and features

Shaolin Boxing has been popular for over 1,000 years, thanks to its excellent effect, unique style and practical combat.

朴实无华。它的套路结构紧凑，动作朴实健壮而敏捷，攻防严密，招势多变。力量的运用灵活而有弹性，着眼于实战不练花架子。

Plain and practical. It is characterized by compact routines, simple, robust and agile movements, tight offense and changeable forms, and flexible and elastic power.

禅拳合一。修习少林功夫者有三层境界：初步境界打习其外表，练其外形，对自己外部形体的锻炼。中层境界为"禅拳合一"，化有形为无形，变有法于无法，无法可依、无招可循。最高境界用心法指导一切，所斗之术为"心"法之争，非"形"法之战。

Meditation and boxing integration. Practicing Shaolin Martial Arts is based on 3 stages: Initial stage focuses on appearance. Middle stage focuses on meditation and boxing integration, making tangible intangible. The highest stage focuses on mind and will.

在演练套路的形式上，有拳打"卧牛之地"一说，这不仅说明演练时场地大小不受限制,在实战中,也能充分利用狭小不利地形,发挥自己的拳技。

Practicing routines are described as "Practicing in a place where the cattle lies", indicating the practicing site is unlimited in size. In actual combat, it is possible to take advantage of a small and unfavorable terrain to play the boxing skills.

"拳打一条线",也是少林拳鲜明的一个特点,各种套路,演练时起落进退,均在一条线上,这是根据实战的需要而设计的。如身法有八要:起、落、进、退、反、侧、收、纵都要求在一条线上活动。

"Boxing along a straight line" is another distinctive feature. Shaolin Boxing can be practiced along a straight line, rising, falling, advancing and retreating all in a line, which is based on the actual needs. The 8 movements cover rising, falling, advancing, retreating, reversing, inclining, closing and releasing.

曲而不曲,直而不直,滚出滚入,运用自如(取南北派之长,练时非长不能达气,对搏时非短不能自顾)。眼法:注目为鹄,以审敌势。身法:起横落顺,掌握重心,不失平衡。步法:进低退高、轻灵稳固,抬腿踢脚,轻如惊鸿、重如泰山,落步生根。在使用方法上要求内"静",外"猛",所谓"守之如处女,犯之如猛虎",并善于借人之力,顺人之势,制人之身,不与来势顶撞,用四两拨千斤之势,以智胜蛮,佯攻而实退,视退而实进,刚柔相济,击其要害。它又以秀如猫、抖如虎、行如龙、动如闪、声如雷,来形容它的变化多端。在动静呼吸运气用气方面,也有自己的特色。拳诀说:拳打十分力,力从气中出,运气贵于缓,用气贵于急,缓急神其术,尽在一呼吸。并以肩与胯、肘与膝、手与足的外三合和心与意、意与气、气与力的内三合之法,内外形成一体。

Great curve appears straight, great straight appears curve, roll in and out, practicing with ease (abstracting merits of north and south schools, long or short practicing dependent on practical situation). Eyes: Gazing the target, judging the rival. Figure: Horizontal rising and longitudinal falling, never losing balance. Stepping: Low advancing and high retreating, ethereal and solid, lifting and kicking as fleeting, and firm falling, requiring as "quiet" as a maid inside and as "fierce" as a tiger outside, leveraging and cleaving, outsmarting, interweaving truth with fiction, integrating simplicity and fortitude, retreating in appearance and advancing in fact, mixing hardness and softness. Fantasticality chopping and changing is characterized by moving as a cat, shaking like a tiger, twisting as a snake, moving like a flash, sounding like a thunder. Vital energy application is unique. Boxing tactics reads: Boxing force comes from vital energy, and vital energy is prepared slowly and applied urgently. Vital energy lies in breathing. Coming force centering on shoulders and hips, elbows and knees, hands and feet, and inner power focusing on mind and will, will and vital energy, vital energy and power structure external and inner integration.

第三节　少林武术的功能价值
Quarter 3　Fitness Effect of Shaolin Martial Arts

少林武术不但在风格特点和技击特点上有独到之处，而且有良好的健身作用。实践证明，长期进行少林武术练习可以改善中枢神经系统的功能。中枢神经系统是调节与支配所有神经系统与器官的枢纽，人类依靠神经系统的活动来适应外界环境的变化，并使体内诸多系统与各个器官的活动，按照要求统一起来。少林武术练习加强了中枢神经系统的作用，对人体的保健起到了很好的作用。少林武术要求注意力集中，呼吸与运动紧密配合，协调锻炼，使大脑皮层运动中枢的活动处在高度亢奋集中状态，皮层的其他部分则因诱导作用而处在广泛的抑制状态，从而对慢性病毒的皮层兴奋灶加强抑制过程，使某些局部的病灶减轻或消失。同时，通过锻炼又进一步增强了对疾病的抵抗能力。此外，长期练习少林武术，还可以提高心脏、血管系统的机能。从少林武术的动作组合来分析，它既包括了全身肌肉关节的快速运动，又包括了意识呼吸和动作呼吸相配合的运动，由于练拳时全身肌肉关节和骨骼往返旋转运动，使动脉血管得到不断舒张，加强了血管舒张神经对血管壁的调节作用，使心脏供血充足，提高心肌的收缩能力。因此，长期练习少林武术对预防各种疾病和动脉硬化可起到积极作用。同时，少林武术动作中的冲拳、劈拳、踢腿、跳跃、深蹲等练习，可增强肌肉的质量和骨骼、关节的活动能力。由于运动离不开肌肉的收缩，而肌肉的收缩与牵引，又引起骨骼、关节的屈与伸，旋内旋外、收缩与放松，这样又对人体起到按摩作用，对增强骨骼、强健关节的柔韧性以及肌肉的肌力和弹性都有明显的作用。总之，长期练习少林拳会给身心健康带来积极的影响。

Shaolin Martial Arts has unique styles and features, and good fitness effects. Practice has proved that long-term Shaolin Martial Arts practicing can improve the function of the central nervous system, which regulates and governs all the nervous systems and organ hubs. Relying on the nervous system activities, human beings adapt to changes in the external environment, and unifying activities of in vivo systems and various organs in accordance with the requirements, strengthening the effect of the central nervous system, playing very good effects on human health. Shaolin Martial Arts requires concentration, close breathing and movement cooperation and coordinated practicing, making the cerebral cortex motor center activities in a highly concentrated and excited state, and other parts in an inhibited state caused by induction, thereby strengthening the inhibition of chronic viral cortical excitability focus, reducing or eliminating some local lesions. At the same time, practicing further enhances resistance to diseases, improves the function of the heart and the vascular system. Based on the analysis of Shaolin Martial Arts movement, it includes rapid movements of the muscles and joints, and sense and movement breathing. In practicing, muscles, joints and bones have rotary movements, constantly expanding the radial artery, strengthening regulation of the vasodilator nerve on the vascular wall, making adequate hearty blood supply adequate, and improving cardiac muscle contraction. Long-term practicing of Shaolin Martial Arts prevents various diseases including arteriosclerosis. Shaolin Martial Arts movements such as punching, chopping, kicking, jumping and squatting can increase muscle quality and bone and joint mobility. Movements are inseparable from muscle contraction, and muscle contraction and dragging cause bone and joint bending and stretching, internal and external rolling, contracting and loosening, playing massage effects, strengthening bone and joint flexibility, muscle strength and flexibility. In short, long-term practicing of Shaolin Martial Arts will have a positive impact on physical and mental health.

第二章 少林基本功和基本技术

Chapter 2 Shaolin Basic Arts and Basic Techniques

第一节 少林桩功(少林基本功法)

Quarter 1 Shaolin Piling(Shaolin Basic Arts)

一、面壁功

第一,两腿交叉,屈膝盘坐,两脚的外侧缘以及臀部着地。两手扶于膝关节上,肩臂放松,头颈正直,两目垂帘(图2-1)。

Section 1 Wall facing and meditating

First, legs cross, sit cross-legged, feet lateral border and buttocks touchdown. Hands hold on knees, arms and shoulders relax, head and neck upright, eyes downward (Figure 2-1).

图2-1(Figure 2-1)

或两掌相叠,掌心向上,放于腹前,右手在上,如此进行练习(图2-2)
Or palms folded supinely, on the abdomen, right hand upwardly (Figure 2-2).

第二章　少林基本功和基本技术

图 2-2(Figure 2-2)

第二,两腿交叉,右腿屈膝,大、小腿均着地;左腿盘于右腿上,左脚放在右腿膝关节处。两手相叠于腹前,右手在上,两肘自然外展,肩部放松,头颈正直,两目垂帘(图 2-3)。

Second, legs cross, right leg crossed, leg and foreleg touchdown; left leg on right leg, left foot on the right knee. Hands folded on the abdomen, right hand upwardly, elbows natural outreach, shoulders relax, head and neck upright, eyes downward (Figure 2-3).

图 2-3(Figure 2-3)

以上是左式。右式则右腿在上,其余同左式(图 2-4)。

That is left posture. Right posture: Right leg upwardly, and the rest the same as the above.(Figure 2-4)

图 2-4(Figure 2-4)

13

二、椅子桩

第一，两脚并拢，两腿屈膝半蹲，大腿接近水平，两臂前举与肩同高、同宽，两手变掌，掌心向下。目视前方（图2-5、图2-6）。

Section 2　Chair piling

First, feet close, bend knees on semi-crouch balance, thigh horizontal, arms forward and apart at the shoulder height and width, change hands into palms, palm center downward, look straight ahead (Figure 2-5 and 2-6).

图2-5(Figure 2-5)　　　　图2-6(Figure 2-6)

第二，做法同上，但两脚分开下蹲，与肩同宽（图2-7、图2-8）。

Second, the same as above, but separate feet and squat, the same wide as the shoulders (Figure 2-7 and 2-8).

图2-7(Figure 2-7)　　　　图2-8(Figure 2-8)

三、丁步桩

两腿并拢屈膝半蹲，右脚全脚着地；左脚尖点地，置于右脚内侧。重心偏向右腿,身体略右转。两手握拳,左拳下栽置于左小腿外侧,拳心向后;右臂屈肘,右拳置于右肩前,拳心向里。头左转。目视左前方(图2-9)。

Section 3 T-step piling

Legs close and bend knees on semi-crouch balance, right foot touchdown, left tiptoe on the floor, place it in the right foot inward. Gravity center on right leg, slightly turn right. Clench fists, thrust downward left fist to lower left leg outward, fist center backward; loosen the right arm and lower the elbow, draw the right fist to the front of the right shoulder, fist center to the inside, head turns left. Look left forward (Figure 2-9).

图 2-9(Figure 2-9)

以上是左丁步桩。右丁步桩则右脚尖点地,其他动作与左丁步桩相似而方向相反(图2-10)。

That is left T-step piling. Right T-step piling, the right tiptoe on the floor, other movements the same as with left T-step piling except direction reverse (Figure 2-10).

图 2-10(Figure 2-10)

第二节 少林基本技术
Quarter 2　Shaolin Basic Techniques

一、手型
Section 1　Hand gesture

1.拳

四指并拢卷屈,拇指紧扣在食指和中指的第二指节上,拳眼向上为立拳（图2-11）。

1.Fist

Four fingers close and bend, clench the thumb on the knuckles of the index finger and middle finger, eye of fist upward refers to vertical fist (Figure 2-11).

图 2-11（Figure 2-11）

拳心向下为俯拳（图2-12）。

Fist center downward refers to horizontal fist (Figure 2-12).

图 2-12（Figure 2-12）

2.掌

柳叶掌:四指并拢伸直,拇指微屈,紧扣于掌外沿(图 2-13 和图 2-14)。

2.Palm

Willow palm: Four fingers close and straight, thumb slightly bends and closely buckles palm outer edge (Figure 2-13 and 2-14).

图 2-13(Figure 2-13)　　　　图 2-14(Figure 2-14)

虎爪掌:五指分开,第一、二指节略向手心弯曲(图 2-15 和图 2-16)。

Tiger claw palm: Five finger apart, the first and second knuckles slightly bend to the palm (Figure 2-15 and 2-16).

图 2-15(Figure 2-15)　　　　图 2-16(Figure 2-16)

3.勾

屈腕,五指之各自第一指节靠拢(图 2-17)。

3.Hook

Bend the wrist and close the first knuckle of each finger (Figure 2-17).

图 2-17(Figure 2-17)

二、拳法

Section 2　Boxing

1.冲拳

预备姿势:身体直立,两拳抱于腰间,肘尖向后,拳心向上。沉肩,挺胸,下颌内收。目视前方(图 2-18)。

1.Punching

Preparation: Stand upright, withdraw fists to the waist, elbow tip backward, fist center upward. Drop shoulders and throw out chest, lower jaw close. Look straight ahead (Figure 2-18).

图 2-18(Figure 2-18)

动作说明:拳由腰间向前猛力冲出成俯拳,力达拳面,然后随着反弹力,小臂微屈(图 2-19~图 2-21)。

Movement descriptions: Punching fists from the waist forward violently into horizontal fist, deliver force to fist face, follow counterforce, forearm slightly bends (Figure 2-19 to 2-21).

图 2-19（Figure 2-19）　　　图 2-20（Figure 2-20）

图 2-21（Figure 2-21）

出立拳时方法同上,唯冲拳后成立拳姿势,肘关节微垂(图 2-22 和图 2-23)。

Vertical fist the same as above, vertical fist only after punching, elbow joints slightly lower (Figure 2-22 and 2-23).

图 2-22（Figure 2-22）　　　图 2-23（Figure 2-23）

2.劈拳

预备姿势:同冲拳的预备姿势(图 2-24)。

2.Chopping

Preparation：The same as punching (Figure 2-24).

图 2-24(Figure 2-24)

动作说明:右拳经腹前,由下向左、向上划弧,再经头上,向右侧劈出成立拳。力达拳轮,拳与肩同高,臂微屈。动作过程眼随视右拳(图 2-25~图 2-27)。

Movement descriptions: Wave right fist in front of the abdomen, draw curve from below to left and upward, then overhead rightward and chop into vertical fist. Deliver the force to palm center reverse side, keep fists at the shoulder's level, arms slightly bend, keep looking at the right fist (Figure 2-25 to 2-27).

图 2-25(Figure 2-25)　　　　图 2-26(Figure 2-26)

图 2-27(Figure 2-27)

3.贯拳

预备姿势:同冲拳的预备姿势(图 2-28)。

3. Swinging

Preparation: The same as punching (Figure 2-28).

图 2-28（Figure 2-28）

动作说明:两拳抱于腰间,右拳由腰间经右侧划弧,前臂内旋,拧腰顺肩,弧形摆击于面前,力达于拳面,拳心向前下方。拳与面部同高。目视右拳方向(图 2-29 和图 2-30)。

Movement descriptions: Withdraw fists to the waist, wave right fist in front of the waist rightward to draw curve, forearm turns inward, twist waist and extend shoulders, swing like a curve, deliver the force to fist face, fist center front downward. Keep fists at face's level. Look at right fist (Figure 2-29 and 2-30).

图 2-29（Figure 2-29）　　图 2-30（Figure 2-30）

4.裹拳

预备姿势:同冲拳预备姿势(图 2-31)。

4. Wrapping

Preparation: The same as punching (Figure 2-31).

图 2-31（Figure 2-31）

动作说明：两拳抱于腰间，右拳从腰间向右、向前、向左摆击。拳与心窝处同高，与胸相距 30 厘米，拳心向里，力达拳面。目视右拳（图 2-32 和图 2-33）。

Movement descriptions: withdraw fists to the waist, swing right fist from waist to right, forward and left. Keep fists at the chest's level, 30cm apart from chest, fist center inward, deliver force to fist face. Look at right fist (Figure 2-32 and 2-33).

图 2-32（Figure 2-32）　　　　图 2-33（Figure 2-33）

5.栽心拳

预备姿势：同冲拳预备姿势（图 2-34）。

5.Striking

Preparation: The same as punching (Figure 2-34).

图 2-34（Figure 2-34）

动作说明:右拳从腰间由下向前、向上屈臂。迅猛发力,力达拳面。拳心朝向胸部,与心窝处同高。下颌内收。目视右拳(图2-35)。

Movement descriptions: Wave right fist from lower waist forward, bend arms upward. Deliver force to fist face violently. Fist center toward the chest, keep fist center at the chest's level. Close lower jaw. Look at right fist (Figure 2-35).

图 2-35(Figure 2-35)

三、掌法

Section 3　Palming

1.推掌

预备姿势:两脚左右开立,与肩同宽。两手变掌置于腰间,肘尖向后,掌心向上(图2-36)。

1.Pushing

Preparation: Feet separate, the same wide as the shoulders. Change hands into palms on the waist, elbow tip backward, supinely (Figure 2-36).

图 2-36(Figure 2-36)

23

动作说明:左臂内旋向前猛力推出成立掌,力达掌根;同时,借反弹力左臂微屈。掌指上翘,并与鼻尖同高。目视左掌(图2-37~图2-39)。

Movement descriptions: Twist left arm inward and violently push forward into raising palm, deliver the force to palm roots, at the same time use counter-force to make left arm slightly bend. Palm fingers upturned and at the nose's level. Look at left palm (Figure 2-37 to 2-39).

图 2-37(Figure 2-37)

图 2-38(Figure 2-38)

图 2-39(Figure 2-39)

2.砍掌

预备姿势:同冲拳预备姿势(图2-40)。

2.Cutting

Preparation: The same as punching (Figure 2-40).

第二章　少林基本功和基本技术

图 2-40（Figure 2-40）

动作说明：两拳抱于腰间，右拳变掌从腰间由下向左上方划弧，经左肩前方，掌心向下（图2-41）。

Movement descriptions: Withdraw fists to the waist, change right fist into palm and draw curve from below to upper left, pass left shoulder, palm center downward (Figure 2-41).

图 2-41（Figure 2-41）

向前、向右屈臂横击，力达于掌外缘。指尖向前，与肩同高。目视右掌（图 2-42 和图 2-43）。

Bend right arm for horizontal striking, deliver the force to palm periphery. Fingertips forward, keep at the shoulder's level. Look at right palm (Figure 2-42 and 2-43).

图 2-42（Figure 2-42）

25

图 2-43(Figure 2-43)

四、肘法

Section 4　Elbowing

1.顶肘

预备姿势:同冲拳预备姿势(图 2-44)。

Preparation: The same as punching (Figure 2-44).

图 2-44(Figure 2-44)

动作说明:两拳抱于腰间,右臂屈肘上抬,与胸同高。右拳置于左胸前,拳心向下(图 2-45)。

1.Butting

Movement descriptions: Withdraw fists to the waist, loosen the right arm and lower the elbow, lift it and keep it at the chest's level. Wave right fist onto left chest, fist center downward (Figure 2-45).

图 2-45(Figure 2-45)

然后以肩带臂向右侧迅猛顶出,力达于肘尖。臂与肩平。目视右前方(图 2-46)。

Butt shoulder and arm rightward violently, deliver the force to elbow tip, keep arm at shoulder's level. Look right front (Figure 2-46).

图 2-46(Figure 2-46)

2.撞肘

预备姿势:同冲拳的预备姿势(图 2-47)。

2.Bump

Preparation: The same as punching (Figure 2-47).

图 2-47(Figure 2-47)

动作说明：右臂屈臂内旋，肘关节由右侧向前猛力撞出，力达于肘。右肩前倾，左肩后牵，肘与肩平。右拳置于胸前，拳心向下。下颌内收。目视肘尖方向（图2-48）。

Movement descriptions: Bend right arm and twist it inward, bump elbow joints forward violently from rightward, deliver the force to elbow. Left shoulder bends forward, left shoulder backward, keep elbow at shoulder's level. Wave right fist onto chest, fist center downward, close lower jaw. Look at elbow tip (Figure 2-48).

图2-48（Figure 2-48）

五、步型

Section 5　Stances

1.弓步（以左弓步为例）

动作说明：由两腿并立姿势起。左脚上前一步，脚尖微内扣，左腿屈膝半蹲（大腿接近水平），膝与脚尖成直线。右腿挺伸直，脚尖内扣（斜向前方），两脚全脚着地。上体正对前方，两手抱拳于腰间。目视前方（图2-49）。弓右腿为右弓步，弓左腿为左弓步。

1.Bow stance (take the left bow stance as an example)

Movement descriptions: Stand at attention. Left foot steps forward, tiptoe slightly buckle inward, left leg bends knees on semi-crouch balance (thigh horizontal), make knee and tiptoe into a straight line. Right leg straight, tiptoe buckles inward (inclined forward), feet touchdown. The upper part of the body right forward, fists against the waist. Look straight ahead (Figure 2-49). Arch right leg for right bow stance, and arch left leg for left bow stance.

图 2-49（Figure 2-49）

2.马步

动作说明：两脚平行开立（约为本人脚长的 3 倍），脚尖正对前方，身体重心落于两脚之间。两手抱拳于腰间。目视前方（图 2-50）。

2.Horse stance

Movement descriptions：Feet parallel and apart（about three times the foot length）, tiptoe right forward, body center of gravity falls between the feet, fists against the waist. Look straight ahead（Figure 2-50）.

图 2-50（Figure 2-50）

3.虚步（以左虚步为例）

动作说明：两脚前后开立，右脚外展约 45°，屈膝半蹲。左脚脚根离地，脚面绷平，脚尖稍内扣，虚点地面。膝微屈，重心落于后腿上。两手叉腰。目视前方（图 2-51）。左脚在前为左虚步，右脚在前为右虚步。

3.Empty stance（Take the left empty stance as an example）

Movement descriptions：Shoulder-width stance. Right foot outreaches about 45°, bend knees on semi-crouch balance. Left heel lifting, instep stretches tight, tiptoe slightly buckles inward, false touching the floor. Knee slightly bends, and gravity center falls on the thigh. Akimbo. Look straight ahead (Figure 2-51). Left foot in front refers to left empty stance, and right foot in front refers to right empty stance.

图 2-51(Figure 2-51)

4.仆步(以左仆步为例)

动作说明:两脚左右开立,右腿屈膝全蹲,大腿和小腿靠紧,臀部接近小腿,右脚全脚着地,脚尖和膝关节外展;左腿挺直平仆,脚尖里扣,全脚着地。两手抱拳于腰间。目视左侧(图 2-52)。仆左腿为左仆步,仆右腿为右仆步。

4.Drop stance (Take left drop stance as an example)

Movement descriptions: Feet separate, right knee bends for spring sitting, legs and foreleg, buttocks close to the foreleg, right foot touchdown, tiptoe and knee outreach, left leg straight and falls forward, tiptoes buckle inward, foot touchdown, fists against the waist. Look leftward (Figure 2-52). Drop left leg refers to left drop stance, and right leg drop refers to right drop stance.

图 2-52(Figure 2-52)

5.歇步(以左歇步为例)

动作说明:两腿交叉相靠全蹲;左脚全脚着地,脚尖外展;右脚前脚掌着地,膝步贴近左腿外侧,臀部坐于右腿接近脚根处,两手抱拳于腰间。目视左前方(图2-53)。左脚在前为左歇步,右脚在前为右歇步。

5.Sitting stance (Take left sitting stance as an example)

Movement descriptions: legs cross and close for spring sitting, left foot touchdown, tiptoes outreach, right sole touchdown, knee close to left leg outside, buttocks on right heel, fists against the waist. Look left forward (Figure 2-53). Left foot in front refers to left sitting stance, and right foot in front refers to right sitting stance.

图 2-53(Figure 2-53)

六、步法

Section 6　Stepping

1.击步

预备姿势:两脚并步站立,两脚尖向前(图2-54)。

1.Beat step

Preparation: Stand up with feet closed, feet pointed forward (Figure 2-54).

图2-54(Figure 2-54)

动作说明:左脚向前迈出一步(图2-55)。

Movement descriptions: Left foot stepping forward (Figure 2-55).

图2-55(Figure 2-55)

重心逐渐由右脚过渡到左脚;然后左脚积极用力上蹬,使身体腾空,在空中右脚从后向前击碰左脚内侧(图2-56)。

Gravity center gradually transfer from right foot to left foot, left foot kicking upward vigorously, jump with right foot hitting left foot inward from back to front in the air (Figure 2-56).

图2-56(Figure 2-56)

身体下降时右脚先落地,左脚随即向前落步。仍然成前后开步站立

（图 2-57）。如此可连续进行练习。

Right foot falls first, and left foot step follows immediately. Resume standing with one foot in the front and the other behind (Figure 2-57). Continuously practice.

图 2-57(Figure 2-57)

2.偷步

预备姿势：两脚左右开立，与肩同宽（图 2-58）。

2.Cheat stance

Preparation: Feet separate, the same wide as the shoulders (Figure 2-58).

图 2-58(Figure 2-58)

动作说明：右腿屈膝提起，经左腿后方向左侧落步，前脚掌着地，脚跟提起。两腿微屈，重心偏向左腿（图 2-59）。

Movement descriptions: Cross and rise right leg, fall on the leftward behind left leg, front sole touchdown, heel rises. Legs slightly bend, gravity center on left leg (Figure 2-59).

图 2-59（Figure 2-59）

3.垫步

预备姿势：两脚前后开步站立（图 2-60）。

3.Skipping stance

Preparation: Stand with one foot in the front and the other behind (Figure 2-60).

图 2-60（Figure 2-60）

动作说明：重心前移至左腿，左膝微屈；右腿屈膝，右脚提于左脚内侧，脚尖上翘，随即在左脚内侧踏地；同时，左脚迅速向前进步，仍成前后开立式（图 2-61 和图 2-62）。

Movement descriptions: Shift gravity center onto left leg, left knee slightly bends, right leg bends, lift right foot into the left foot inward, with tiptoes upturned, fall in the left foot inward, at the same time left foot advances quickly. Resume standing with one foot in the front and the other behind (Figure 2-61 and 2-62).

第二章　少林基本功和基本技术

图 2-61(Figure 2-61)

图 2-62(Figure 2-62)

4.换跳步

预备姿势：两脚前后开步站立(图 2-63)。

4.Jump and change stance

Preparation：Stand with one foot in the front and the other behind (Figure 2-63).

图 2-63(Figure 2-63)

动作说明：重心移至左腿，右腿屈膝向前提摆，脚尖外展(图 2-64)。

Movement descriptions：The center of gravity shift to left leg, cross and swing right leg forward, tiptoes outreach (Figure 2-64).

图 2-64(Figure 2-64)

左腿蹬地跳起,身体腾空,左腿屈膝小腿后举,右腿自然下垂(图2-65)。

Jump with left leg, bend left leg and lift foreleg, right leg naturally droops (Figure 2-65).

图 2-65(Figure 2-65)

然后右脚落地,支撑重心,左腿下落,并向前方落步,成前后开立步(图2-66)。

Right foot falls to support gravity center, left leg falls and move forward, and stand with one foot in the front and the other behind (Figure 2-66).

图 2-66(Figure 2-66)

5.弹子步

预备姿势:两脚开步站立,两脚脚尖正对前方(图2-67)。

5.Marble stance

Preparation: Stand with one foot in the front and the other behind (Figure 2-67).

图 2-67(Figure 2-67)

动作说明:左脚在前,成前后开立步,两腿微屈,重心移向左脚,右脚脚跟提起(图 2-68)。

Movement descriptions: Stand with left foot in the front and right leg behind, legs slightly bend, shift gravity center onto left foot, raise right heel (Figure 2-68).

图 2-68(Figure 2-68)

身体继续前移,右脚前脚掌擦地上抬(图 2-69)。

Continue moving forward, rub the front right sole against the floor and raise (Figure 2-69).

图 2-69(Figure 2-69)

随后右腿自然前摆,向前上一步,仍成前后开立步。如此两腿交替练习(图 2-70~图 2-72)。

Right leg naturally swings forward, advance and resuming standing with one foot in the front and the other behind. Legs alternative practicing (Figure 2-70 to 2-72).

图 2-70(Figure 2-70)

图 2-71(Figure 2-71)

图 2-72　Figure 2-72

第三章　少林武术操
Chapter 3　Shaolin Martial Arts Exercise

第一节　套路动作名称
Quarter 1　Routine Names

1. 预备势(Preparation)
2. 手型变换(Hand form conversion)
3. 罗汉眉(Arhat eyebrow)
4. 乌龙盘柱(Black dragon coils column)
5. 迎面腿(Head-on kicking)
6. 飞脚望月(Back leg flying kicking)
7. 马步冲拳(Horse-riding punching)
8. 跨虎登山(Riding and striding)
9. 单飞燕(Single flying swallow)
10. 收势(Closing)

第二节　套路动作图解
Quarter 2　Figures of Routine Movements

一、预备势

Section 1　Preparation

1.并立式

两脚并拢,身体直立。目视前方(图3-1)。

1.Parallel posture

Close feet, stand upright. Look straight ahead (Figure 3-1).

图 3-1(Figure 3-1)

2.抱拳式

两手抱拳于腰间。目视前方(图 3-2)。

2.Holding fists posture

Fists against the waist. Look straight ahead (Figure 3-2).

图 3-2(Figure 3-2)

二、手型变换(2×8 拍)

Section 2　Hand form conversion (2×8 shots)

1.迎门炮(前冲拳)

左脚向左跨半步;同时,两拳向前冲出,拳与肩同高,拳心相对,两臂平直。目视前方(图 3-3)。

1.Cannon right overhead

(Front punching): Left foot strides half a step leftward, at the same time, punch fists forward, keep fists at the shoulder's level, fist centers against each other, arms straight. Look straight ahead (Figure 3-3).

图 3-3(Figure 3-3)

2.定心掌(双立掌)

两肘向下微屈,两拳同时变掌,塌腕上挑成立掌,掌心斜相对,指尖与肩同高。目视前方(图 3-4)。

2.Centering palm

(Double vertical palms): Bend elbows downward slightly, change fists into palms, bend and lift wrists into vertical palms, palm centers against each other, keep fingertip at shoulder's level. Look straight ahead (Figure 3-4).

图 3-4(Figure 3-4)

3.挂金钟(勾手分臂)

两掌变勾;同时,分别向左右两侧直臂摆击,勾尖向下,勾顶比肩略高,头左转。目视左前方(图 3-5)。

3.Bell hanging (Hooking arms)

Change palms into hooks, at the same time lift arms leftward and rightward, hook tip downward, hook top is slightly higher than the shoulder, turn left. Look leftward (Figure 3-5).

图 3-5(Figure 3-5)

4.抱拳式

左脚收回,并步直立;同时,两勾手变拳收抱腰间成抱拳式。目视前方(图 3-6)。

4.Holding fists posture

Close left foot, step touch upright, at the same time, change hooks into fists onto the waist into holding fists posture. Look straight ahead (Figure 3-6).

图 3-6(Figure 3-6)

5.5~8 拍同 1~4 拍的动作,要求相同,左右对称。

5.5 to 8 shots the same as 1 to 4 shots in requirements, bilaterally symmetrical.

三、罗汉眉(2×8 拍)

Section 3　Arhat eyebrow (2×8 shots)

1.剑诀手(伸臂侧指)

左脚向左跨半步,两拳变剑指,分别向左右两侧伸臂平指,两手心均向下。目视前方(图 3-7)。

1.Sword fingers (Arm stretching)

Move left foot half a step leftward, change fists into sword fingers, stretch arms leftward and rightward, and hand centers downward. Look straight ahead (Figure 3-7).

图 3-7(Figure 3-7)

2.罗汉眉(转身屈臂)

以左脚跟、右脚掌为轴,向左后转体 180°成交叉步;同时,两臂屈肘,左右剑指指向眉梢,指尖距离眉梢 10 厘米,手心向前。目视前方(图 3-8)。

2.Arhat eyebrow (turn and bend arms)

Turn left heel with right sole as the axis, turn leftward and backward 180° into crossed steps, at the same time, bend elbows, left and right sword fingers point brow tips, fingertip 10cm away from brow tip, hand centers forward. Look straight ahead (Figure 3-8).

图 3-8(Figure 3-8)

3.剑诀手(伸臂侧指)

以左脚跟、右脚掌为轴,向右后转体180°,两手分别向左右两侧伸臂平指,两手心均向下。目视前方(图3-9)。

3.Sword fingers (Arm stretching)

Turn rightward and backward 180° with left heel and right sole as the axis, stretch hands leftward and rightward, hand centers downward. Look straight ahead (Figure 3-9).

图3-9(Figure 3-9)

4.抱拳式

左脚收回,并步直立,两手变拳收于腰间。目视前方(图3-10)。

4.Holding fists posture

Close left foot, step touch upright, change hands into fists against waist. Look straight ahead (Figure 3-10).

图3-10(Figure 3-10)

5.5~8 拍同 1~4 拍的动作,要求相同,左右对称。

5.5 to 8 shots the same as 1 to 4 shots in requirements, bilaterally symmetrical.

四、乌龙盘柱(2×8 拍)

Section 4 Black dragon coils column (2×8 shots)

1.怀中抱月(腹前托掌)

左脚向左跨半步,两拳变掌托于腹前,右掌在上,两掌心均向上。目视前方(图 3-11)。

1.Hold moon in arms (protect palm in front of abdomen)

left foot strides half a step leftward, change fists into palms against the abdomen, right palm on, palm center were upward. Look straight ahead (Figure 3-11).

图 3-11(Figure 3-11)

2.云盖顶(架掌勾手)

右掌经面前向上屈肘横架于头顶上方,掌心向上;同时,左掌变勾手经左腿侧向后、向下摆击,勾尖向上,臂伸直,贴于体侧,挺胸收腹摆头。目视左方(图 3-12)。

2.Cloud covers peak (Hooking palms)

Shift right palm upward and bend elbow overhead, supinely, at the same time, shift left palm backward via left leg and change it into hook, hook tip upward, arms straight, downward, throw out chest and turn. Look leftward (Figure 3-12).

图 3-12(Figure 3-12)

3.龙盘柱(俯身攀腿)

上体向下俯身,右手由上向下伸臂扣于左腿外踝部,左臂伸直保持勾手,上体尽力靠近左腿(两腿要伸直),头左转。目视斜上方(图 3-13)。

3.Dragon coils column (Bend and stretch legs)

The upper part of the body downward, right hand stretches downward and buckles on left ankle, left arm straight and maintain hooking, the upper part of the body close to left leg (legs straight), turn left. Look obliquely upward (Figure 3-13).

图 3-13(Figure 3-13)

4.抱拳式

上体抬起,左脚收回,并步直立,两手变拳收抱腰间。目视前方(图 3-14)。

4.Holding fists posture

The upper part of the body rises, close left foot, step touch upright, change hands into fists and close them against waist. Look straight ahead (Figure 3-14).

第三章　少林武术操

图 3-14(Figure 3-14)

5.5~8 拍同 1~4 拍的动作,要求相同,左右对称。

5.5 to 8 shots the same as 1 to 4 shots in requirements, bilaterally symmetrical.

五、迎面腿(2×8 拍)

Section 5　Head-on kicking (2×8 shots)

1.护胸捶(屈臂勾拳)

左脚向前上半步,右脚尖点地,重心移向左腿;右拳屈臂上勾,拳与肩同高,肘部贴肋。目视前方(图 3-15)。

1.Chest protection fist (Bend arm and hook fist)

Left foot strides forward half a step, right tiptoe touchdown, shift gravity center to the left leg, bend right fist and make it hook upward, keep fists at the shoulder's level, elbow against ribs. Look straight ahead (Figure 3-15).

图 3-15(Figure 3-15)

47

2.迎面腿(摆臂正踢)

右腿伸直,勾脚尖,向体前额部上踢;同时,右拳向下经右腿侧后摆,拳心向上;支撑腿要直,身体保持正直。目视前方(图3-16和图3-17)。

2.Head-on kicking (Swing arm and kick forward)

Right leg straight, hook tiptoes, kick toward the forehead, at the same time, swing right fist downward by the leg, fist center upward, supporting leg straight, keep upright. Look straight ahead (Figure 3-16 and 3-17).

图3-16(Figure 3-16)　　图3-17(Figure 3-17)

3.护胸捶(屈臂勾拳)

右脚向下后落,脚尖点地,重心在左腿;同时,右臂前摆屈肘上勾,拳与肩同高,肘部贴肋。目视前方(图3-18)。

3.Chest protection fist (Bend arm and hook fist)

Right foot falls downward and backward, tiptoes touch the floor, shift gravity center to the left leg, at the same time, swing the right arm forward and bend elbow to hook upward, keep fists at the shoulder's level, elbow against ribs. Look straight ahead (Figure 3-18).

图3-18(Figure 3-18)

4.抱拳式

左脚后收,并步直立,右拳收抱腰间,成抱拳式(图 3-19)。

4.Holding fists posture

Close left foot backward, step touch upright, Close right fist against waist, into holding fists posture (Figure 3-19).

图 3-19(Figure 3-19)

5.5~8 拍同 1~4 拍的动作,要求相同,左右对称。

5. 5 to 8 shots the same as 1 to 4 shots in requirements, bilaterally symmetrical.

六、飞脚望月(2×8 拍)

Section 6　Back leg flying kicking (2×8 shots)

1.左飞脚(左拍脚)

左腿由屈到伸,向前、向上摆踢,脚面绷平,脚与胸同高;同时,左拳变掌,向前上伸臂,在面前拍击左脚面,拍声响亮;上体要正,两腿要直,右拳抱腰间。目视前方(图 3-20)。

1.Left flying kicking (Left foot patting)

Bend and stretch left leg, swing and kick forward and upward, instep stretches tight, keep foot at chest'level, at the same time, change left fist into palm, stretch arm forward and upward, pat left instep ringingly, the upper part of the body upright, legs straight, right fist against the waist. Look straight ahead (Figure 3-20).

图 3-20(Figure 3-20)

2.抱拳式

左脚落回原地,并步直立,左手变拳收抱腰间成抱拳式(图 3-21)。

2.Holding fists posture

Left foot falls back, step touch upright, change left hand into fist against the waist into holding fists posture (Figure 3-21).

图 3-21(Figure 3-21)

3.右飞脚(右拍脚)

与左飞脚动作相同,左右对称(图 3-22)。

3.Right flying kicking (Right foot patting)

The same as left flying kicking in movements, bilaterally symmetrical (Figure 3-22).

图 3-22(Figure 3-22)

4.抱拳式

右脚落回原地,并步直立,右手变拳收抱腰间成抱拳式(图3-23)。

4.Holding fists posture

Right foot falls back, step touch upright, change tight hand into fist against the waist into holding fists posture (Figure 3-23).

图3-23(Figure 3-23)

5.右望月式(右后拍脚)

左腿屈膝,小腿由右腿后向斜上撩踢,脚底向上(支撑腿要直);上体右拧,右拳变掌拍击左脚底;左拳变掌向左上摆击至头左上方,掌心斜向上,臂微屈。目视拍脚处(图3-24)。

5.Right back leg posture (Rightward and backward foot patting)

Bend left knee, foreleg arc kicks from back of the right leg, sole upward (supporting leg straight). Twist the upper part of the body rightward, change right fist into palm and pat left sole. Change left fist into palm and swing it leftward and upward overhead, palm center obliquely upward, bend arms slightly. Look at foot patting (Figure 3-24).

图3-24(Figure 3-24)

6.抱拳式

左脚落回原地,并步直立,两手变拳收抱腰间成抱拳式(图3-25)。

6.Holding fists posture

Left foot falls back, step touch upright, change hands into fists against the waist into holding fists posture (Figure 3-25).

图3-25(Figure 3-25)

7.左望月式(左后拍脚)

与右望月式动作相同,左右对称(图3-26)。

7.Left back leg posture (Leftward and backward foot patting)

The same as right back leg posture in movements, bilaterally symmetrical (Figure 3-26).

图3-26(Figure 3-26)

8.抱拳式

右脚落回原地,并步直立,两手变拳收抱腰间成抱拳式。目视前方(图3-27)。

8.Holding fists posture

Right foot falls back, step touch upright, change hands into fists against the waist into holding fists posture. Look straight ahead (Figure 3-27).

图 3-27(Figure 3-27)

七、马步冲拳(2×8 拍)

Section 7　Horse-riding punching (2×8 shots)

1.迎门炮(马步冲拳)

左脚向左跨一步,半蹲成马步;同时,两拳向前冲出,拳心相对,两臂平直。目视前方(图 3-28)。

1.Cannon right overhead (Horse-riding punching)

Left foot strides a step leftward, partly squat into the horse stance, at the same time, punch fists forward, fist centers against each other, arms straight. Look straight ahead (Figure 3-28).

图 3-28(Figure 3-28)

2.护胸捶(胸前抱拳)

下肢不动,两臂屈肘,两拳收抱于胸前,拳心向里,两肘贴肋。目视前方(图 3-29)。

2.Chest protection fist（Holding fists in front of the chest）

Legs still, bend elbows, close fists against the chest, palm center inward, elbows against the ribs. Look straight ahead (Figure 3-29).

图 3-29（Figure 3-29）

3.单鞭式（马步侧冲拳）

下肢不动,两肘分别左右外摆,带动小臂快速向体侧摆击,拳心向下,两臂平直。目视左拳方向(图 3-30)。

3.Single whipping posture（Horse-riding inclined punching）

Legs still, raise and swing elbows leftward and rightward respectively, driving forearm incline and stretch quickly, fist center downward, arms straight. Look at the left fist (Figure 3-30).

图 3-30（Figure 3-30）

4.抱拳式

左脚收回原地,并步直立,两拳收抱腰间成抱拳式。目视前方(图3-31)。

4.Holding fists posture

Left foot falls back, step touch upright, fists against the waist into holding fists posture. Look straight ahead (Figure 3-31).

图 3-31(Figure 3-31)

5.5~8拍同1~4拍的动作,要求相同,左右对称。

5.5 to 8 shots the same as 1 to 4 shots in requirements, bilaterally symmetrical.

八、跨虎登山(2×8拍)

Section 8　Riding and striding (2×8 shots)

1.平心掌(弓步推掌)

左脚向左一步,上体微左转成左弓步;同时,右拳变勾向上、向左、向下搂至右后侧,勾尖向上,直臂贴身。当勾手搂经腹前时,左拳变掌经右小臂内侧向左前推出成立掌,指尖与肩同高,掌沿向前,臂微屈。目视左掌方向(图3-32)。

1.Leveling palm(Bow stance pushing)

Left foot strides a step leftward, the upper part of the body slightly turn left and into left bow stance, at the same time, change right fist into hook and brush upward, leftward, downward and rightward and backward, hook-tip upward, arms straight. Hook and brush against the abdomen, change left fist into palm and push leftward and forward via right forearm inner side into vertical palm, keep fingertip at shoulders' level, palm center rightward, and bend arms slightly. Look at left palm (Figure 3-32).

图 3-32（Figure 3-32）

2. 平心掌（转身推掌）

以两脚掌为轴，身体右转，成右弓步；同时，左掌向右经体前向下变勾搂至左后侧，勾尖向上，直臂贴身；当勾手搂经腹前时，右手变掌经左小臂内侧向右前推出成立掌，指尖与肩同高，掌沿向前，臂微屈。目视右掌方向（图3-33）。

2. Leveling palm

(Turn and push): Turn right with soles as the axis, into right bow stance, at the same time, change left palm into hook, and brush it downward and leftward, hook-tip upward, and arms straight. Hook and brush against the abdomen, change right fist into palm and push rightward and forward via left forearm inner side into vertical palm, keep fingertip at shoulders' level, palm center leftward, and bend arms slightly. Look at right palm (Figure 3-33).

图 3-33（Figure 3-33）

3. 平切掌（转身横掌）

以两脚掌为轴，身体左转，成左弓步；同时，右掌向左经体前向上变勾搂至右后侧，勾尖向上，直臂贴身；当勾手搂经腹前时，左手变掌经右小臂内侧向左前横掌推出,掌心斜向下,掌与胸同高,臂微屈,肘尖向外。目视左掌方向(图 3-34)。

3.Leveling cutting palm

(Turn and form horizontal palm): Turn left with soles as the axis, into left bow stance, at the same time, change right palm into hook, and brush it downward and rightward, hook-tip upward, and arms straight. Hook and brush against the abdomen, change left fist into palm and push leftward and forward via right forearm inner side palm center slantingly downward, keep palm at shoulders' level, bend arms slightly, palm center outward. Look at left palm (Figure 3-34).

图 3-34(Figure 3-34)

4.抱拳式

左脚收回原地,并步直立,两手变拳收抱腰间成抱拳式(图 3-35)。

4.Holding fists posture

Left foot falls back, step touch upright, change hands into fists against the waist into holding fists posture (Figure 3-35).

图 3-35(Figure 3-35)

5.5~8拍同1~4拍的动作,要求相同,左右对称。

5.5 to 8 shots the same as 1 to 4 shots in requirements, bilaterally symmetrical.

九、单飞燕(2×8拍)

Section 9　Single flying swallow (2×8 shots)

1.右击手炮(蹲身击拳)

左脚向左跨一步,右脚向上提起,两臂侧摆,右手是拳,左手变掌(图3-36)

1.Right hitting cannon

(Squat and hit): Left foot strides a step leftward, lift right foot swing arms, change right hand into fist, left hand into palm (Figure 3-36).

图3-36(Figure 3-36)

上动不停,右脚紧随落地,振脚下蹲(重心偏左腿,上体要直);同时,两臂向内回收在膝前合击,右拳面扣击左掌。目视前下方(图3-37)。

Keep moving, right foot falls, vibrate foot and squat (shift gravity center to left leg, the upper part of the body straight), at the same time, close arms inward and punch in front of the knees, right fist face buckles and left palm hits. Look front downward (Figure 3-37).

图3-37(Figure 3-37)

2.右单飞燕(腾空拍脚)

左脚蹬地跳起,随即右腿伸直向右前上方45°摆击,右脚面绷平,右拳变掌拍击右脚面,左手抱拳于腰间。目视拍脚方向(图3-38)。

2.Right single flying swallow(Jumping foot patting)

Left foot falls and jumps, right leg straight and swings rightward and forward 45°, right instep stretches tight, change right fist into palm and pat right instep, left hand holds fist against the waist. Look at foot patting (Figure 3-38).

图3-38(Figure 3-38)

3.左击手炮(蹲身击拳)

右脚向右下方体侧落步,左脚向上提起,两臂侧摆,左手是拳,右手变掌(图3-39)。

3.Left hitting cannon(Squat and hit)

Right foot strides a step rightward, lift left foot, swing arms, change left hand into fist, right hand into palm (Figure 3-39).

图3-39(Figure 3-39)

上动不停,左脚紧随落地,振脚下蹲(重心偏右腿,上体要直);同时,两臂向内回收在膝前合击,左拳面扣击右掌。目视前下方(图3-40)。

Keep moving, left foot falls, vibrate foot and squat (shift gravity center to right leg, the upper part of the body straight), at the same time, close arms inward and punch in front of the knees, left fist face buckles and right palm hits. Look front downward (Figure 3-40).

图 3-40(Figure 3-40)

4.左单飞燕(腾空拍脚)

右脚蹬地跳起,随即左腿伸直向左前上方45°摆击,左脚面绷平,左拳变掌拍击左脚面,右手抱拳于腰间。目视拍脚方向(图3-41)。

4. Left single flying swallow (Jumping foot patting)

Right foot falls and jumps, left leg straight and swings leftward and forward 45°, left instep stretches tight, change left fist into palm and pat left instep, right hand holds fist against the waist. Look at foot patting (Figure 3-41).

图 3-41(Figure 3-41)

5.右击手炮(蹲身击拳)

左脚向左下方体侧落步,右脚向上提起,两臂侧摆,右手是拳,左手变掌(图 3-42)。

5.Right hitting cannon (Squat and hit)

Left foot strides a step leftward, lift right foot, swing arms, change right hand into fist, left hand into palm (Figure 3-42).

图 3-42(Figure 3-42)

上动不停,右脚紧随落地,震脚下蹲(重心偏左腿,上体要直);同时,两臂向内回收在膝前合击,右拳扣击左掌。目视前下方(图 3-43)。

Keep moving, right foot falls, vibrate foot and squat (shift gravity center to left leg, the upper part of the body straight), at the same time, close arms inward and punch in front of the knees, right fist buckles left palm. Look front downward (Figure 3-43).

图 3-43(Figure 3-43)

6.5~8拍同1~4拍动作,要求相同,左右对称。

6.5 to 8 shots the same as 1 to 4 shots in requirements, bilaterally symmetrical.

注:第二个八拍做到口令6(即右单飞燕,图3-38)后,下接。

Note: The second 8 shots until 6 (namely right single flying swallow, Figure 3-38), followed by.

7.右震脚

上动不停,左脚落地后右脚向左脚内侧落地震脚,右腿微屈;同时,左脚提起,脚尖向下,右手变拳由前向下成右下击,左拳由腰间向左上摆击。目视右手(图3-44)。

7. Right stamping

Keep moving, Left foot falls, right foot falls and stamps the inner side of the left foot, slightly bend right leg, at the same time, bend and raise left foot, tiptoes downward, change right hand into fist and hit from front downward into rightward and downward, swing left fist rightward and upward from the waist. Look at right hand (Figure 3-44).

图3-44(Figure 3-44)

8.坐山势(马步架栽拳)

上动不停,左脚向左落成马步,右拳向上、向左摆,架于头右前上方;左拳下栽于左膝上,左臂微屈外展;头随右拳上摆的同时左摆。目视左前方发"威"声(图3-45)。

8.Sitting-at-mountain pose (Horse-riding stance thrusting)

Keep moving, left foot falls leftward into the horse-riding stance, swing right fist upward and leftward, thrust right-front overhead, thrust left fist downward against left knee, slightly bend and outreach left arm, swing right fist upward and the head leftward. Look leftward and cry "Wei" (Figure 3-45).

图 3-45(Figure 3-45)

十、收势

Section 10　Closing

1.左脚向右收步,两脚并拢,身体直立;两拳收于腰间成抱拳势。目视前方(图 3-46)。

1.Close left foot rightward, close feet, stand upright; close fists against the waist into holding fists. Look straight ahead (Figure 3-46).

图 3-46(Figure 3-46)

2.两拳变掌,两臂伸直下垂于身体两侧,成立正姿势(图3-47)。

2.Change fists into palms, arms straight and hang against both sides into standing at attention (Figure 3-47).

图 3-47(Figure 3-47)

第四章 少林基本动作(少林十八势)

Chapter 4　Shaolin Basic Movements (Shaolin 18 Forms)

第一节　套路动作名称

Quarter 1　Routine Names

第一段　步型

Section 1　Stances

1. 弓步斜形(Bow stance and cut obliquely)
2. 马步单鞭(Horse-riding single whip)
3. 虚步格掌(Empty stance parrying palm)
4. 仆步切掌(Drop stance cutting palm)
5. 歇步冲拳(Sitting stance punching)

第二段　腿法

Section 2　Kicking

1. 正踢腿(Forward kicking)
2. 外摆腿(Swinging kick)
3. 里和腿(Inward crescent kicking)
4. 单拍脚(Single foot patting)
5. 低弹腿(Low toe kicking)
6. 侧踹腿(Side sole kicking)
7. 勾踢腿(Low hook kicking)
8. 后蹬腿(Back heel kicking)
9. 蝎子尾(后扫腿)(Scorpion tail (Back sweeping))

10.前扫腿(Front sweeping)

第三段　跳跃动作
Section 3　Jumping

1.腾空二起脚(Jumping front kicking)

2.腾空旋风脚(Jumping whirlwind kicking)

3.腾空外摆莲(Jumping lotus swinging)

4.收势(Closing)

第二节　套路动作图解
Quarter 2　Figures of Routine Movements

第一段　步型
Section 1　Stances

1.弓步斜形

预备姿势:两脚左右开立,与肩同宽。两拳抱于腰间,肘尖向后,拳心向上。目视前方(图4-1)。

1.Bow stance and oblique cutting

Preparation: Feet separate, the same wide as the shoulders, withdraw fists to the waist, elbow tip backward, fist center upward. Look straight ahead (Figure 4-1).

图4-1(Figure 4-1)

第四章 少林基本动作(少林十八势)

动作说明:左脚向左横跨半步,脚尖斜向前方成左弓步,两拳变掌向左下方伸出,掌心斜向上。目视两掌(图4-2)。

Movement descriptions: Move left foot half a step leftward horizontally, tiptoe angled forward into left bow stance, change fists into palms and stretch out to bottom left, palm diagonally upward. Look at palms (Figure 4-2).

图4-2(Figure 4-2)

重心后移成半马步,两掌变拳,屈肘抱于胸前,拳心向里。两肘紧贴胸部。目视左前方(图4-3)。

Shift gravity center backward to half horse-riding, change palms into fists, bend elbows onto the chest, fist center inward. Make elbows close to the chest. Look left forward (Figure 4-3).

图4-3(Figure 4-3)

右脚尖内扣,积极用力蹬地,拧腰,身体向左转,成左弓步。两拳内旋,并分别向前后冲出。臂微屈,拳心向下。目视右手方向(图4-4)。

Right tiptoe buckles inward, stomp vigorously, twist waist, and turn left into left bow stance. Fists turn inwards, and punch forward and backward separately. Bend arms slightly, fist center downward. Look right (Figure 4-4).

图 4-4（Figure 4-4）

右弓步斜形的练习方法与左弓步斜形相同（图 4-5 和图 4-6）。

Right bow stance and oblique cutting practicing methods is the same as left bow stance and oblique cutting (Figure 4-5 and 4-6).

图 4-5（Figure 4-5）　　　　图 4-6（Figure 4-6）

2.马步单鞭

预备姿势：同弓步斜形预备姿势（图 4-7）。

Preparation: The same as bow stance and oblique cutting (Figure 4-7).

图 4-7（Figure 4-7）

2.Horse-riding single whip

动作说明：左脚向左侧跨步，两脚间距为脚长的 3 倍，脚尖正对前方；同

第四章 少林基本动作(少林十八势)

时,两拳变掌,由腰间向下伸出。两腿屈蹲,两掌变拳,屈肘抱于胸前。拳心向里,两肘关节紧贴胸部(图4-8和图4-9)。

Movement descriptions: Left foot strides leftward, spacing between feet 3 times foot length, tiptoe right forward, at the same time change fists into palms, stretch downward from the waist, bend legs and squat, change palms into fists, bend elbows onto the chest, fist center inward, make elbows joints close to the chest (Figure 4-8 and 4-9).

图4-8(Figure 4-8)   图4-9(Figure 4-9)

两腿继续屈蹲使大腿接近水平;同时,两拳由胸前分别向两侧屈臂撑出。两拳与肩同高,拳心向下。目视左拳(图4-10)。

Resume bending and squatting and make thigh horizontal, at the same time, bend arms and make fists stretch to both sides separately. Keep fists at the shoulder's level, fist center downward. Look at left fist (Figure 4-10).

图4-10(Figure 4-10)

如此可在行进间进行练习(图4-11~图4-13)。

Practicing while advancing (Figure 4-11 to 4-13).

图4-11(Figure 4-11)

图4-12(Figure 4-12)

图4-13(Figure 4-13)

3.虚步格掌

预备姿势:两脚左右开立,与肩同宽。两拳抱于腰间,肘尖向后,拳心向上。目视前方(图4-14)。

3.Empty stance parrying palm

Preparation: Feet separate, the same wide as the shoulders. Withdraw fists to the waist, elbow tip backward, fist center upward. Look straight ahead (Figure 4-14).

图4-14(Figure 4-14)

第四章 少林基本动作(少林十八势)

动作说明:右脚向右前方上半步,重心偏向右脚,两腿微屈。身体微右转,两掌经腰间上穿至胸前,两掌心斜向上,小臂微屈,右掌在左臂内侧。目视前方(图 4-15)。

Movement descriptions: Right foot strides half a step to right front, shift gravity center to right foot, and slightly bend legs. Slightly turn right, shift palms to the chest through the waist, palm centers obliquely upward, slightly bend forearms, make right palm in the left arm inward. Look straight ahead (Figure 4-15).

图 4-15(Figure 4-15)

重心移至右腿,右腿屈膝半蹲;左腿向左前方上步,左脚脚尖内扣并虚步点地。同时,左掌向左翻掌横格,掌心向前,左臂微屈,右掌扶于左臂内侧。目视左掌方向(图 4-16)。

Shift gravity center to right leg, bend right knee on semi-crouch balance. Left leg strides to the left front, left tiptoes buckle inward and empty stance on the floor. At the same time, turn left palm and swing leftward, palm center forward, slightly bend left arm, hold right palm at left arm inward. Look at left palm (Figure 4-16).

图 4-16(Figure 4-16)

如此,可行进间左右练习(图 4-17、图 4-18)。

71

Practicing while advancing (Figure 4-17 and 4-18).

图 4-17(Figure 4-17)　　　　图 4-18(Figure 4-18)

4.仆步切掌

预备姿势：两脚左右开立，与肩同宽。两拳抱于腰间，肘尖向后，拳心向上。目视前方(图 4-19)。

4.Drop stance cutting palm

Preparation: Feet separate, the same wide as the shoulders. Withdraw fists to the waist, elbow tip backward, fist center upward. Look straight ahead (Figure 4-19).

图 4-19(Figure 4-19)

动作说明：右脚向前上步，脚尖外展，两腿微屈；同时，两拳变掌，由腰间向胸前伸出，指尖向上，右掌在前，掌心向前，左掌附于右小臂内侧。目视右掌(图 4-20)。

Movement descriptions: Right foot strides forward, tiptoes outreach, slightly bend legs, at the same time change fists into palms, stretch to the chest from the waist, fingertips upward, right palm in the front, palm center forward, left palm against right forearm inward. Look at right palm (Figure 4-20).

图 4-20(Figure 4-20)

重心移至右腿,左脚屈膝提起,右臂外旋,掌心翻向上,左掌附于右臂上方(图 4-21)。

Shift gravity center to right leg, cross and raise left foot, right arm rotates outward, palm center turns upward, left palm against upper right arm(Figure 4-21).

图 4-21(Figure 4-21)

右腿屈膝全蹲,膝和脚尖稍外展,左脚向前方铲出,腿伸直,脚尖内扣成仆步;同时,右掌变拳,右牵于腰间,左掌以小指侧为力点顺势向前推出,至左脚背上方。目视左掌(图 4-22)。

Bend right knee for spring sitting, knee and tiptoe outreach slightly, left foot outreaches forward, legs straight, tiptoe buckles inward into drop stance. At the same time, change right palm into fist, right palm against the waist, shift force to left little finger inward and push forward until left instep. Look at left palm (Figure 4-22).

73

图 4-22（Figure 4-22）

左右练习方法相同，可行进间练习（图 4-23～图 4-25）。

Left and right practicing methods are the same, practicing while advancing (Figure 4-23 to 4-25).

图 4-23（Figure 4-23）　　　图 4-24（Figure 4-24）

图 4-25（Figure 4-25）

5.歇步冲拳

5.Sitting stance punching

预备姿势：两脚左右开立，与肩同宽。两拳抱于腰间，肘尖向后，拳心向上。目视前方（图 4-26）。

Preparation: Feet separate, the same wide as the shoulders. Withdraw fists to the waist, elbow tip backward, fist center upward. Look straight ahead (Figure 4-26).

第四章 少林基本动作(少林十八势)

图 4-26(Figure 4-26)

动作说明:左脚向左侧上半步,脚尖外展,两腿微屈;同时,身体左转,左拳变掌由腰间向前、向左、向后搂手。目视左掌(图 4-27)。

Movement descriptions: Left foot strides half a step leftward, tiptoes outreach, slightly bend legs. At the same time, turn left, change left fist into palm and brush forward, to the left and backward from the waist. Look at left palm (Figure 4-27).

图 4-27(Figure 4-27)

身体继续左转,两腿交叉屈膝全蹲成左歇步;同时,左手搂手变拳抱于腰间,右拳由腰间迅猛冲出,拳心向下,力达拳面。目视右拳(图 4-28)。

Continues turning left, cross leg for spring sitting and into left sitting stance. At the same time, change left hand into fist against the waist, push right fist from the waist violently, fist center downward, and deliver force to fist face. Look at right fist (Figure 4-28).

图 4-28(Figure 4-28)

75

左右练习方法相同,可行进间练习(图4-29和图4-30)。

Left and right practicing methods are the same, practicing while advancing (Figure 4-29 and 4-30).

图4-29(Figure 4-29)　　　　图4-30(Figure 4-30)

第二段　腿法

Section 2　Kicking

1.正踢腿(以右腿为例)

1.Forward kicking (Take the right leg for an example)

预备姿势:两脚左右开立,与肩同宽。两拳抱于腰间,肘尖向后,拳心向上。目视前方(图4-31)。

Preparation: Feet separate, the same wide as the shoulders. Withdraw fists to the waist, elbow tip backward, fist center upward. Look straight ahead (Figure 4-31).

图4-31(Figure 4-31)

动作说明:左脚向前上半步,重心移向左腿,右脚向前一步;同时,右臂屈肘向前、向上勾拳,拳至右肩前,拳心向里(图4-32)。

Movement descriptions: Left foot strides forward half a step, shift gravity center to the left leg, right foot strides forward a step, at the same time bend the right arm and lower the elbow, hooking forward and upward, shift the fist to the right shoulder, fist center inward (Figure 4-32).

图 4-32(Figure 4-32)

右脚脚尖勾起向前上方前额处踢摆;右臂伸直,向下劈拳(图4-33)。

Hook right tiptoe forward to the forehead, right arm straight, chopping downward (Figure 4-33).

图 4-33(Figure 4-33)

右脚下落,脚尖点地;同时,两拳收抱于腰间。目视前方(图4-34)。

Right foot falls, and tiptoes touch the floor, at the same time, close fists onto the waist. Look straight ahead (Figure 4-34).

图 4-34(Figure 4-34)

77

如此可行进间两腿交替进行练习(图 4-35 至图 4-37)。

Alternate practicing while advancing (Figure 4-35 to 4-37).

图 4-35(Figure 4-35)　　　图 4-36(Figure 4-36)

图 4-37(Figure 4-37)

2.外摆腿(以右腿为例)

预备姿势:两脚左右开立,与肩同宽。两拳抱于腰间,肘尖向后,拳心向上。目视前方(图 4-38)。

2.Swinging kick (Take the right leg for an example)

Preparation: Feet separate, the same wide as the shoulders. Withdraw fists to the waist, elbow tip backward, fist center upward. Look straight ahead (Figure 4-38).

图 4-38(Figure 4-38)

第四章　少林基本动作(少林十八势)

动作说明:左脚向前上步,左腿微屈;同时,两拳变掌由腰间向前上方抢手,左掌与下颌同高,肘关节微屈,右掌贴于左小臂上。目视左掌(图4-39)。

Movement descriptions: Left foot strides forward, bend left leg slightly, at the same time, change fists into palms, grab upward and forward from the waist, keep left palm at lower jaw's level, slightly bend elbow joints, right palm against left forearm. Look at left palm (Figure 4-39).

图 4-39(Figure 4-39)

右脚尖勾起,里扣,向前、向左、向上经面前向右踢腿;同时,左右两掌由右向左在面前依次迎击右脚背(图4-40)。

Hook right tiptoes, buckle inward, kick forward, to the left, upward and right; at the same time, left and right palms resist right instep from right to left (Figure 4-40).

图 4-40(Figure 4-40)

随即右腿向右、向下、向后下落,右脚尖着地;同时,双掌变拳收抱腰间。目视前方(图4-41)。

Right leg falls to the right, downward and backward, right tiptoes touchdown, at the same time, change palms into fists onto the waist. Look straight ahead (Figure 4-41).

图 4-41(Figure 4-41)

如此行进间两腿交替进行练习(图 4-42~图 4-44)。

Alternate practicing while advancing (Figure 4-42 to 4-44).

图 4-42(Figure 4-42)

图 4-43(Figure 4-43)　　图 4-44(Figure 4-44)

3.里和腿(以右腿为例)

预备姿势:两脚左右开立,与肩同宽,身体正直。两手握拳抱于腰间。目视前方(图 4-45)。

3.Inward crescent kicking (Take the right leg for an example)

Preparation: Feet separate, the same wide as the shoulders. Keep upright. Hold fists against the waist. Look straight ahead (Figure 4-45).

图 4-45(Figure 4-45)

动作说明:左脚向左跨步,脚尖外摆,随之身体左转;同时,左手变掌向前上穿出,掌指与鼻尖同高,拇指侧向上。目视左掌(图 4-46)。

Movement descriptions: Left foot strides to the left, outreach tiptoes, turn left, at the same time, change left hand into palm thrusting forward, keep fingers at the nose's level, thumb upward. Look at left palm (Figure 4-46).

图 4-46(Figure 4-46)

右脚脚尖勾起,里扣,并向右、向前、向上、向左踢摆,脚掌与左手在面前合击(图 4-47)。

Hook right tiptoes, buckle them inward, kick to the right, forward and upward, punch the sole with the left hand (Figure 4-47).

81

图 4-47（Figure 4-47）

在右脚将下落之际,右臂屈肘抬起,拳至肩上;身体继续左转,右腿屈膝成独立势。右拳经肩前下栽拳于体侧,拳心向后;左掌变拳屈臂。拳至肩前,拳心向里。目视右方(图 4-48 和图 4-49)。

Right foot falls, bend the right arm and lower the elbow, shift fists onto shoulders. Turn left, cross right leg and stand on one leg. Shift fist against the side through the shoulder, fist center backward; change left palm into fist and bend the arm. Shift fist on to the shoulder, fist center inward. Look right (Figure 4-48 and 4-49).

图 4-48（Figure 4-48）   图 4-49（Figure 4-49）

如此行进间两腿交替进行练习(图 4-50~图 4-53)。

Alternate practicing while advancing (Figure 4-50 to 4-53).

图 4-50（Figure 4-50）   图 4-51（Figure 4-51）

第四章 少林基本动作(少林十八势)

图 4-52（Figure 4-52） 图 4-53（Figure 4-53）

4.单拍脚

预备姿势：同正踢腿(图 4-54)。

4.Single foot patting

Preparation：The same as forward kicking (Figure 4-54).

图 4-54（Figure 4-54）

动作说明：左脚向前上步，重心移至左腿，右脚脚跟提起。目视前方(图 4-55)。

Movement descriptions：Left foot strides forward, shift gravity center to left leg, and lift right foot. Look straight ahead (Figure 4-55).

图 4-55（Figure 4-55）

重心移至左腿，右脚由后方向前、向上直腿摆起，脚面绷直；同时，右拳变掌，由腰间向前拍击右脚面(图 4-56)。

83

Shift gravity center to left leg, swing right foot forward and upward from back, stretch out instep, at the same time, change right fist into palm, pat right instep from the waist (Figure 4-56).

图 4-56(Figure 4-56)

右腿击响后直腿向前落地；同时，右掌变拳抱于腰间。目视前方（图 4-57）。

Pat right leg and fall straight forward fall, at the same time, change right palm into fist against the waist. Look straight ahead (Figure 4-57).

图 4-57(Figure 4-57)

如此在行进间两腿交替进行练习(图 4-58 和图 4-59)。

Alternate practicing while advancing (Figure 4-58 and 4-59).

图 4-58(Figure 4-58)　　图 4-59(Figure 4-59)

5.低弹腿

预备姿势:同正踢腿(图 4-60)。

5.Low toe kicking

Preparation: The same as forward kicking (Figure 4-60).

图 4-60(Figure 4-60)

动作说明:左脚向前上一步,重心前移。目视前方(图 4-61)。

Movement descriptions: Left foot strides forward, gravity center forward. Look straight ahead (Figure 4-61).

图 4-61(Figure 4-61)

重心向前移至左脚;同时,右脚向前提膝。大腿接近水平时,小腿迅速向前猛力弹击,力达脚尖(图 4-62 和图 4-63)。

Shift gravity center to left foot, move right foot forward and lift knee. Thigh horizontal, foreleg stretches forward violently, deliver the force to tiptoes (Figure 4-62 and 4-63).

图 4-62(Figure 4-62)   图 4-63(Figure 4-63)

右脚前落,脚尖着地。目视前方(图4-64)。

Right foot falls forward, tiptoes touchdown. Look straight ahead (Figure 4-64).

图4-64(Figure 4-64)

如此行进间两腿交替进行练习(图4-65~图4-67)。

Alternate practicing while advancing (Figure 4-65 to 4-67).

图4-65(Figure 4-65)　　图4-66(Figure 4-66)

图4-67(Figure 4-67)

6.侧踹腿

预备姿势:同正踢腿(图4-68)。

6.Side sole kicking

Preparation: The same as forward kicking (Figure 4-68).

第四章　少林基本动作(少林十八势)

图 4-68（Figure 4-68）

动作说明：左脚向前上步，重心移向左腿，脚尖外展；同时，身体微向左转，右臂屈肘向上举起，拳与肩同高。目视右拳方向（图 4-69）。

Movement descriptions: Left foot strides forward, shift gravity center to the left leg, tiptoes outreach, at the same time, slightly turn left, bend and lift right elbow, keep fist at the shoulder's level. Look at right fist (Figure 4-69).

图 4-69（Figure 4-69）

身体继续向左微转，右脚脚尖勾起里扣，右脚屈膝向前、向上提起，膝同腰高（图 4-70）。

Slightly turn to left, make right tiptoe hook and buckle inward, cross right foot forward, lift knee and keep it at the waist's level (Figure 4-70).

图 4-70（Figure 4-70）

右腿向右侧迅速猛力伸出，力达脚跟，与腰同高，上体向左侧微倾；同时,右拳经胸腹前向右斜下栽拳于裆前;左臂屈肘向上抬起,拳面与左腮相对。肘尖向下。目视右腿方向(图 4-71)。

Stretch right leg to the right side violently, deliver the force to heel and keep it at the waist's level, the upper part of the body leans to the left side, at the same time, shift the right fist to the right in front of the abdomen and thrust it to the front of the crotch, bend left elbow upward, make fist face against left cheek, elbow pointed downward. Look at right leg (Figure 4-71).

图 4-71(Figure 4-71)

如此在行进间两腿交替进行练习(图 4-72 至图 4-74)。

Alternate practicing while advancing (Figure 4-72 to 4-74).

图 4-72(Figure 4-72)　　图 4-73(Figure 4-73)

图 4-74(Figure 4-74)

7.鸡型步

预备姿势:同正踢腿(图 4-75)。

7.Chicken type step

Preparation: The same as kicking (Figure 4-75).

图 4-75(Figure 4-75)

动作说明：左脚向前上步，重心移向左脚，左膝关节微屈，左脚尖稍外展；同时，身体微向左转；右拳变掌屈肘上摆，至左肩前，指尖向上，掌心向外（图 4-76）。

Movement descriptions: Left foot strides forward, shift gravity center to left foot, slightly bend left knee, slightly outreach left tiptoes, at the same time, slightly turn left, change right fist into palm and bend elbow and swing it upward until the left shoulder, fingertips upward, palm center outward (Figure 4-76).

图 4-76(Figure 4-76)

重心移至左腿，右脚前掌向前擦地提膝内扣、勾起；同时，上体向右微转，右掌向下、向右、向后砍掌于右髋旁，力达小指侧；左拳变掌，屈肘上摆至右肩前，指尖向上，掌心向外。目视右侧（图 4-77 和图 4-78）。

Shift gravity center to left leg, make right sole forward and touchdown and lift and buckle inward the knee, hook upward, at the same time, the upper part of the body slightly turn to the right, right palm center downward, make the right palm cut backward, to the right and left beside the right hip, deliver the force to little finger, change left fist into palm, bend the elbow and swing it to the front of the right shoulder, fingertips upward, palm center outward. Look right (Figure 4-77 and 4-78).

图4-77(Figure 4-77)　　　　图4-78(Figure 4-78)

如此行进间两腿交替进行练习(图4-79和图4-80)。

Alternate practicing while advancing (Figure 4-79 and 4-80).

图4-79(Figure 4-79)　　　　图4-80(Figure 4-80)

8.后蹬腿

预备姿势:同正踢腿(图4-81)。

8.Back heel kicking

Preparation: The same as kicking (Figure 4-81).

第四章 少林基本动作(少林十八势)

图 4-81(Figure 4-81)

动作说明:左脚向前上步,迅速屈膝下蹲,右膝顺势下跪于左脚内侧(但膝不触地面),右脚跟提起,重心偏于右腿,上体微前倾;同时,上体微右转,右拳变掌向后下方伸出,虎口与脚跟相对;左拳变掌向上摆至右肩前,指尖向上,掌心向外。目视右后方(图 4-82)。

Movement descriptions: Left foot strides forward, bend the knees and squat quickly, make right knee kneel inside the left foot (but the knee does not touch the floor), lift right foot, shift gravity center to right leg, the upper part of the body slightly forward, at the same time, the upper part of the body slightly turn right, change right fist into palm and have it stretch backward, make the part between the thumb and the forefinger against the heel, change the left fist into palm and swing it upward to the right shoulder, fingertips upward, palm center outward. Look right rear (Figure 4-82).

图 4-82(Figure 4-82)

右脚伸起,上体继续前倾,右腿顺势由屈而猛力向后伸出,力达脚跟,脚尖向右下方;同时,右手顺势屈肘向蹬腿方向伸出。目视蹬腿方向(图 4-83)。

stretch upward the right foot, the upper part of the body forward, stretch out right leg backward violently, deliver the force to heel, shift tiptoes to the bottom right, at the same time, bend right elbow and stretch it out for heel kicking. Look in heel kicking direction (Figure 4-83).

图 4-83（Figure 4-83）

如此行进间两腿交替进行练习（图 4-84 和图 4-85）。

Alternate practicing while advancing（Figure 4-84 and 4-85）

图 4-84（Figure 4-84）

图 4-85（Figure 4-85）

9.蝎子尾（后扫腿）

预备姿势：同前面第一势的弓步斜形（图 4-86）。

9.Scorpion tail（Back sweeping）

Preparation：The same as bow stance and oblique cutting of section 1（Figure 4-86）.

第四章 少林基本动作(少林十八势)

图 4-86(Figure 4-86)

动作说明:左脚向左迈半步,以左脚掌为轴,身体向后转体180°;同时,右脚掌擦地,右腿屈膝,小腿向右后撩起,右拳变掌向右后平搂手(图 4-87)。

Movement descriptions: Move left foot half a step leftward horizontally. Turn backward 180° with the left sole as the axis, at the same time, right sole touchdown, cross right leg, shift foreleg to the right tease and upward, change right fist into palm and push it to the right side and backward (Figure 4-87).

图 4-87(Figure 4-87)

接着,身体继续向右起,右腿提膝,脚尖绷直内扣;同时,右掌向下插掌至小腿内侧,右小臂与腿内侧贴紧,右掌背紧贴内髁,指尖向下;左拳变掌架于头上方,掌心斜向上。目视前方(图 4-88 和图 4-89)。

Straighten to the right side, lift right knee, keep straight and buckle inward tiptoes, at the same time, thrust right palm into foreleg inner side, make right forearm against leg inner side, right dorsal palm against inner condyle, fingertip downward, change left fist into palm and maintain it overhead, palm center obliquely upward. Look straight ahead (Figure 4-88 and 4-89).

图 4-88(Figure 4-88)　　　图 4-89(Figure 4-89)

如此行进间两腿交替进行练习(图 4-90~图 4-93)。

Alternate practicing while advancing (Figure 4-90 to 4-93).

图 4-90(Figure 4-90)　　　图 4-91(Figure 4-91)

图 4-92(Figure 4-92)　　　图 4-93(Figure 4-93)

10.前扫腿

预备姿势:两脚左右开立,与肩同宽。两拳抱于腰间,肘尖向后,拳心向上。目视前方(图 4-94)。

10.Front sweeping

Preparation: Right leg spring sitting, left leg straight into left drop stance, hands against the crotch, fingertips against each other, look in crouching direction (Figure 4-94).

图 4-94(Figure 4-94)

动作说明:右腿向后退一步,身体右转,左脚尖点地收于右脚内侧,两腿下蹲成丁字步;同时,两拳变掌向身体右侧摆掌。目视右掌(图 4-95)。

Movement descriptions: Shift gravity center to the left leg, spring sitting, turn left with the left sole as the axis, right sole touchdown, right leg straight and sweep forward and to the left (half-circle), shift hands to the crotch (Figure 4-95).

图 4-95(Figure 4-95)

左脚向前一步成弓步;同时,两臂向腹前摆击,右掌变拳迎击左掌,左掌拍击在右拳背上。目视前方(图 4-96)。

Keep moving, right leg sweeps to the left (half-circle), lean to the right side and forward, hands touchdown (Figure 4-96).

图 4-96(Figure 4-96)

上动不停,两脚向前垫步跳起,右拳收于腰间,左掌附于右拳上。目视前方(图4-97)。

Keep moving, left foot jumps and falls. Left leg jumps and right foot sweeps backward and forward and becomes right drop stance. Look in crouching direction (Figure 4-97).

图4-97(Figure 4-97)

上动不停,右腿落地,左腿伸直成右仆步;同时,左掌向左脚面上切掌,右拳抱至腰间。目视左掌(图4-98)。

Keep moving. Right leg falls and left leg stretches into right drop stance, while left palm touches the left foot, right fist against the waist. Look at left palm (Figure 4-98).

图4-98(Figure 4-98)

重心移至左腿,右脚掌擦地向前、向左扫腿(前半周);同时,身体右前倾,右拳变掌同左掌同时向前撑地。目视右脚(图4-99)。

Shift gravity center to left leg, right feet stretches leftward and sweep to the left (the first half circle); at the same time, body bends right forward, shift right fist to palm and and push against ground together with left palm. Look at right foot (Figure 4-99).

第四章 少林基本动作(少林十八势)

图 4-99(Figure 4-99)

紧接上动,在右腿扫至左腿前时两掌撑地,左脚蹬地跳起,使右腿从左腿下方朝左后方掏扫(后半周)置于身体右侧。目视右脚(图 4-100)。

Keep moving. Left leg jumps while right leg sweeps to the position of left leg, palms against ground, to make the right leg below left leg and continues sweeping to left (the second half circle). Look at right foot (Figure 4-100).

图 4-100(Figure 4-100)

上动不停,身体上起,左脚向前脚尖点地收于右脚内侧。屈膝下蹲成丁字步;同时,两臂向右前方摆掌。目视右掌(图 4-101)。

Keep moving. Stand up and left toe touches against ground at the middle of right foot. Then bend knees on semi-crouch balance into T-step, at the same time, both arms moves right forward. Look at right palm (Figure 4-101).

图 4-101(Figure 4-101)

如此行进间交替进行练习(图 4-94~图 4-101)。

Alternate practicing while advancing (Figure 4-94 to 4-101).

第三段　跳跃动作

Section 3　Jumping

1.腾空二起脚

预备姿势:两脚左右开立,与肩同宽。两拳抱于腰间,肘尖向后,拳心向上。目视前方(图 4-102)。

1.Jumping front kicking

Preparation: Feet separate, the same wide as the shoulders. Withdraw fists to the waist, elbow tip backward, fist center upward. Look straight ahead (Figure 4-102).

图 4-102(Figure 4-102)

动作说明:左脚向左前方上一步,右脚跟进扣在左脚内侧,两腿屈膝半蹲,身体微向左转;同时,两拳变掌,左掌贴膝下插于左膝外侧,掌心向外,右掌护于左肩前方,掌心向外。目视前方(图 4-103)。

Movement descriptions: Left foot strides to the left front, right heel strides and buckles in left foot inner side, bend knees on semi-crouch balance, slightly turn left, at the same time, change fists into palms, left palm against the knee and inserts in left knee outside, palm center outward, right palm protects left shoulder front, palm center outward. Look straight ahead (Figure 4-103).

第四章　少林基本动作(少林十八势)

图 4-103(Figure 4-103)

两脚同时蹬地,身体腾空,左脚向前上弹踢,脚面绷直,右腿自然下垂。右手变拳抱于腰间,左掌向前插掌,拍左脚脚面,成左二起脚(图 4-104)。

Feet fall simultaneously, jump, the left foot kicks forward, keeping instep straight, right leg naturally drops. Change right hand into palm against the waist, left palm thrusts forward, slap left instep into left front kicking (Figure 4-104).

图 4-104(Figure 4-104)

身体下落,右脚尖着地,左腿向右前方落步,两腿微屈,右手抱拳于腰间不动,左掌在胸前向左格掌,臂微屈,指尖向上(图 4-105)。

Fall and right tiptoes touchdown, left leg falls to the right front, slightly bend legs, change right hand into fist and keep it against waist, shift left palm to the left in front of the chest, bend arms slightly, fingertips upward (Figure 4-105).

图 4-105（Figure 4-105）

左脚向前半步,右脚跟进扣在左脚内侧,两脚并拢,屈膝半蹲,身体微向右转;左掌由胸前贴膝下插于左膝外侧;右拳变掌向左上方摆击护于左肩前方,掌心向外。头要正,下颌内收。目视前方(图4-106)。

Left foot strides half a step forward, right heel strides and buckles at the inner side of the left foot, bend knees on semi-crouch balance, slightly turn right; insert left palm to the left knee outside the front of the chest, change right fist into palm swings upward to protect the front of the left shoulder, palm center outward. Keep upright, close lower jaw. Look straight ahead (Figure 4-106).

图 4-106（Figure 4-106）

接做右二起脚时,方法同上,但左右相反(图4-107 和图 4-108)。

Right front kicking is the same as above, but change right into left (Figure 4-107 and 4-108).

第四章 少林基本动作(少林十八势)

图 4-107(Figure 4-107)

图 4-108(Figure 4-108)

2.腾空旋风脚

预备姿势:同二起脚(图 4-109)。

2.Jumping whirlwind kicking

Preparation: The same as front kicking (Figure 4-109).

图 4-109(Figure 4-109)

动作说明:右脚向后退一步。身体右倾,挺胸,塌腰成右弓步;同时,两拳变成虎爪掌,左掌下按置于左髋上方,掌心向上;右臂屈肘向上,右掌置于右额旁,掌心向外。目视左侧前方(图 4-110)。

Movement descriptions: Right foot strides one step to the back, lean rightward, throw out chest, turn waist downward into the right bow stance. At the same time change hands into "tiger claw" palms. Press left palm against front hip, palm center slantingly upward. Bend the right arm and lower the elbow, right palm against right forehead, palm center outward. Look leftward ahead (Figure 4-110).

图 4-110（Figure 4-110）

两腿屈膝半蹲，重心下降，左膝内扣，身体略向右转，两臂自然向右侧摆动，上身微向前倾。目视前下方（图 4-111）。

Bend knees on semi-crouch balance, gravity center decreases, left knee buckles inward, slightly turn right, arms swing naturally rightward, the upper part of the body slightly leans forward. Look front downward (Figure 4-111).

图 4-111（Figure 4-111）

接着，重心移至右腿，右腿蹬地，并随之向左转体，左腿离地上摆，两臂由右侧自然向下、向左上方摆动，上体立起（图 4-112）。

Shift gravity center to the right leg, right leg falls, and subsequently turns left, left leg swings upward, arms naturally swing downward and upper leftward from rightward, stand upright (Figure 4-112).

第四章 少林基本动作(少林十八势)

图 4-112(Figure 4-112)

右腿继续用力向上蹬起,身体腾空,并向左后方转体 180°,右臂侧举,右腿做里合腿,左手在面前迎击右脚掌,左腿自然下垂(图 4-113)。

Right leg kicks upward, jump, turn left rear 180°, lift right arm, close right leg inward, use left hand to resist the right sole, left leg naturally drops (Figure 4-113).

图 4-113(Figure 4-113)

身体在空中继续转体 180°,两脚左右依次落地,成开步站立,两腿微屈,身体略向左转,两手变虎爪掌,在体前相抱,掌心上下斜相对(图 4-114)。

Turn 180° in the air, feet fall in turn, stand with feet separated, slightly bend legs, slightly turn left, change hands into "tiger claw" palms, hold each other, palm centers diagonally opposite to each other (Figure 4-114).

图 4-114(Figure 4-114)

重心移向右腿成右弓步,两掌经胸前交叉,右掌在外,并向左右两侧分

103

掌。身体微右倾,并略向左转,成望月式(图 4-115)。收势后,可连续练习。

Shift gravity center to the right leg into the right bow stance, cross palms in front of the chest, right palm outside, spread palms leftward and rightward. Lean slightly rightward and turn leftward, into back leg (Figure 4-115). Continuous practicing.

图 4-115(Figure 4-115)

3.腾空外摆莲

预备姿势:同二起脚(图 4-116)。

3.Jumping lotus swinging

Preparation: The same as as front kicking (Figure 4-116).

图 4-116(Figure 4-116)

动作说明:右脚向前一步,身体左转 180°,两腿屈膝前弓,成左弓步,两手变掌向前抢出,左掌与下颌同高,掌心向上,右掌贴于左小臂内侧,身体正直。目视前方(图 4-117)。

Movement descriptions: Right foot strides forward a step, turn left 180°, bend legs forward into the left bow stance, change hands into palms and stretch them forward, keep left palm at lower jaw's level, supinely, right palm against

第四章 少林基本动作(少林十八势)

the left forearm inward, keep upright. Look straight ahead (Figure 4-117).

图 4-117(Figure 4-117)

弓步抢手后,身体向右后转体,两腿微屈,右脚脚尖外展,重心在两腿之间,两臂自然向后摆。右臂屈肘与肩同高,右臂屈肘摆于胸前,掌心向下(图 4-118)。

Bow stance forms, turn rightward, slightly bend legs, right tiptoes outreach, shift gravity center between the legs, arms swinging naturally backward. Bend right arm and lower the elbow, keep it at shoulder's level, bend right arm and lower the elbow in front of the chest, palm center downward (Figure 4-118).

图 4-118(Figure 4-118)

重心移至右腿,两臂自然向右、后、上方摆臂。目视前方(图 4-119)。

Shift gravity center rightward leg, and naturally swing arms rightward, backward and upward. Look straight ahead (Figure 4-119).

图 4-119(Figure 4-119)

右腿用力积极上蹬,身体腾空,并向右后转体。右腿做外摆,摆置面前,左、右手向左依次击拍右脚脚面,左腿自然下垂(图4-120)。

Right leg kicks upward vigorously, jump, and turn rightward. Swing right leg outside, use hands to pat right instep leftward into left bow stance, left leg naturally drops (Figure 4-120).

图4-120(Figure 4-120)

左脚落地,右腿向右后方摆落,成左弓步。两手变掌,由腰间向前方伸出,成弓步抢手(图4-121)。可连续练习。

Left foot falls, right leg swings rightward and backward and falls, into the left bow stance. Change hands into palms, stretch forward from the waist, into the bow stance (Figure 4-121). Continuous practicing.

图4-121(Figure 4-121)

4.收势

左脚收回原地,并步直立,两手臂下垂还原成预备势的姿势(图4-122和图4-123)。

第四章　少林基本动作(少林十八势)

4.Closing

Left foot returns to the original place, step touch and stand firm, arms fall and restore preparation posture (Figure 4-122 and 4-123).

图 4-122(Figure 4-122)　　图 4-123(Figure 4-123)

注：因少林基本动作是在行进间运行时练习，所以每一式的结束动作就是第二式的起始动作。特加以说明。

Note: Shaolin basic movements are practiced in advancing therefore each closing movement is the starting movement of the next.

第五章　少林小洪拳24式
Chapter 5　24-Shaolin Xiaohong Boxing（24 Forms）

第一节　套路名称
Quarter 1　Routine Names

第一段
Section 1

1. 预备势（Preparation）
2. 怀中抱月（Holding moon in arms）
3. 白云盖顶（White cloud covering peak）
4. 上步一掌（Advancing and palming）
5. 抱拳缩身（Holding fists and shrinking）
6. 上步抢手（Stepping forward and grabbing）
7. 外摆莲（Lotus swinging）
8. 弓步斜形（Bow stance and oblique cutting）
9. 压臂缩身（Pressing arm and shrinking）
10. 上步迎面腿（Stepping forward and head-on kicking）
11. 弓步顶心肘（Bow stance butting elbow）
12. 云顶七星（Cloud butting seven-star）
13. 马步单鞭（Horse-riding single whipping）

第二段
Section 2

14. 单飞脚（Single flying kicking）

15.海底捞月(Pick up the moon from the sea bottom)

16.震脚击手炮(Stamping and hitting cannon)

17.掏心捶(Digging and pounding)

18.打虎式(Tiger subduing)

19.下栽捶(Downward planting)

20.云顶砸拳(Butting and smashing downward)

21.旋飞脚(Whirling and lying kicking)

22.冲天炮(Punching upward)

23.老虎大张嘴(Tiger mouth-opening)

24.迎面搬掌(Head-on palming)

25.坐山势(Mountain riding)

26.收势(Closing)

第二节　套路动作图解
Quarter 2　Figures of Routine Movements

第一段

Section 1

1.预备势

(1)两脚并立,两臂自然下垂于身体两侧,挺胸收腹,成立正姿势。目视前方(图5-1)。

1.Preparation

(1) Feet parallel, arms fall naturally, stand at attention. Look straight ahead (Figure 5-1).

图 5-1(Figure 5-1)

(2)两臂屈肘向上提,两掌变拳抱腰间;同时,左脚向左一步,与肩同宽。目视前方(图5-2)。

(2)Bend elbows upward, change palms into fists against the waist, at the same time, left foot strides one step leftward, the same wide as the shoulders. Look straight ahead (Figure 5-2).

图5-2(Figure 5-2)

2.怀中抱月

两肘外展,两拳变掌相叠贴于腹部,掌心均向上,右掌在上。目视前方(图5-3)。

2.Holding moon in arms

Outreach elbows, change fists into palms folded against abdomen, palm centers upward, right palm upward. Look straight ahead (Figure 5-3).

图5-3(Figure 5-3)

3.白云盖顶

右掌经胸前屈臂架于头前上方,掌心斜向上;左臂伸直下垂,紧贴体侧,指尖向下,掌心向后。目视左方(图5-4)。

3.White cloud covering peak

Bend right arm and shift the palm overhead in front of the chest, palm center obliquely upward, left arm straight and drooping, against the left side, fingertips downward, palm center backward. Look leftward (Figure 5-4).

图 5-4(Figure 5-4)

4.上步一掌

身体左转,左脚向左一步屈膝成左弓步,右掌外旋向左、向下压经体前变拳收至腰间;同时,左掌向上经左胸前向前推出成立掌,指尖与颏同高。目视左掌(图5-5)。

4.Advancing and palming

Turn left, left foot advances into the left bow stance, at the same time, swing right palm leftward and downward, change into fist against the waist. Right palm passes in front of the left chest, push left palm into vertical palm above right palm, and keep fingertips at chin's level. Look at left palm (Figure 5-5).

图 5-5(Figure 5-5)

5.抱拳缩身

身体右转,重心移向右腿,左脚收至右脚内侧,两腿屈膝半蹲成左丁步;同时,右拳变掌,掌心向上经左小臂下向上屈肘变拳收抱于右肩前,掌心向内;左臂屈肘,左掌变拳回收经胸前向身体右侧摆臂栽拳,拳心向后。目视左前方(图 5-6)。

5.Holding fists and shrinking

Turn right, shift gravity center to right leg, close left foot to right foot inner side, bend knees on semi-crouch balance into left T step, at the same time, thrust right center toward left forearm bottom, bend elbow and change palm into fist against right shoulder, palm center against shoulder. Bend left arm into elbow, pass left palm in front of the chest and change palm into fist against right arm inner side, thrust the arm and strike by the side, palm center backward. Look left forward (Figure 5-6).

图 5-6(Figure 5-6)

6.上步抢手

(1)两腿上起,身体左转;同时,左拳向上,右拳向下收抱胸前,两拳心向上。目视前方(图 5-7)。

6.Stepping forward and grabbing

(1)Stand still, turn left, close fists against the chest, and palm centers upward. Left fist in the front, right fist inside the left elbow, elbows against the ribs. Look straight ahead (Figure 5-7).

图 5-7(Figure 5-7)

(2)上动不停,左脚向前上一步成弓步;同时,两拳变掌向前抢出,左掌在前与胸同高,右掌在后置于左小臂内侧,掌心向上。目视左掌(图 5-8)。

(2) Keep moving, left foot forward into the bow stance, at the same time, change fists into palms and stretch them forward, bend arms slightly, keep left palm at the chest's level, right palm inside left forearm, palm center upward. Look at left palm (Figure 5-8).

图 5-8(Figure 5-8)

7.外摆莲

身体重心向前移至左腿,右脚向前、向上、向右(向外)踢摆;同时,左右两掌在右脚向外摆踢于体前时依次向左(向里)迎击脚面。目视拍击脚(图 5-9)。

7.Lotus swinging

Right leg kicks forward, leftward, upward and rightward, leg straight, instep stretches tight, the foot passes and hands resist instep leftward, slightly bend and stabilize the supporting leg. Look foot patting (Figure 5-9).

图 5-9(Figure 5-9)

8.弓步斜形

(1)右脚向前落步,身体左转,两腿屈膝下蹲成马步;同时,两臂屈肘,两掌变拳收至胸前,拳心向里,两肘贴肋。目视前方(图5-10和图5-11)。

8.Bow stance and oblique cutting

(1)Right leg strides a big step forward, turn left, slightly squat, at the same time bend elbows, change hands into fists to the front chest, fist center inward, elbows against the ribs. Look straight ahead (Figure 5-10 and 5-11).

图 5-10(Figure 5-10)　　　　图 5-11(Figure 5-11)

(2)上动不停,身体右转成右弓步;两拳随身体右转的同时由胸前分别向两侧冲击,拳心均向下,与肩同高,两臂微屈,两拳眼相对。目视左拳(图5-12)。

(2)Throw right tiptoes outward, turn right, shift gravity center to right leg into the right bow stance, at the same time, turn and punch fists to both sides from the front chest, fist centers downward, keep them at shoulders' level, and slightly bend arms, fist centers against each other. Look at the left fist (Figure 5-12).

图 5-12(Figure 5-12)

第五章　少林小洪拳24式

9.压臂缩身

身体左转,右脚向后收至左脚内侧,屈膝下蹲成右丁步;同时,左臂屈肘收于左肩前,拳心向内。右臂屈肘向前经左臂上方向下摆击收于体侧,拳心向后。目视右前方(图5-13和图5-14)。

9.Pressing arm and shrinking

Close right foot to left foot inward, turn left and partly squat into T step, at the same time, bend left elbow, close left fist against left shoulders. Fist center against the shoulder, bend right elbow and turn it leftward and depress the forearm, arms straight and fall against both sides, fist center backward. Look right forward (Figure 5-13 and 5-14).

图 5-13(Figure 5-13)

图 5-14(Figure 5-14)

10.上步迎面腿

(1)身体右转上起,右腿向前上步;同时,右拳向上收抱腰间,左拳向上摆击于左肩前。目视左拳(图5-15)。

10.Stepping forward and head-on kicking

(1)Legs stretch upward, turn right, right leg strides one step rightward, at the same time, bend the right arm and lower the elbow, right fist against the waist. Look at left fist (Figure 5-15).

图 5-15(Figure 5-15)

115

（2）上动不停,左腿向前、向上摆踢;左臂屈肘以左拳臂为力点向下劈拳置于左胯旁,拳心向上。目视前方(图5-16)。

(2) Left leg swings and kicks forward and upward, leg straight, tiptoes hook upward, touch the forehead, bend left elbow and shift force to left fist and arm, smash forward and downward, and make it fall against the left hip, fist center upward. Look straight ahead (Figure 5-16).

图 5-16(Figure 5-16)

11.弓步顶心肘

左脚向前下落成左弓步;同时,右臂向胸前盘肘前顶,拳心向下;左臂向上收于胸前再向下、向上架于头顶上方,拳心向前。目视前方(图5-17)。

11. Bow stance butting elbow

Left foot falls forward into the bow stance, at the same time, bend right arm to the front chest and bend elbow and but, fist center downward, slightly bend left arm and parry upward in front of the chest, swing fist overhead, fist center forward. Look straight ahead (Figure 5-17).

图 5-17(Figure 5-17)

12.云顶七星

(1)右脚向前一步,身体上起,右拳收抱腰间。目视前方(图5-18)。

12.Cloud Butting Seven-star

(1) Right leg strides one step forward, rise, close right fist against the waist. Look straight ahead (Figure 5-18).

图5-18(Figure 5-18)

(2)上动不停,右脚向前上一步,左拳由头顶向后、向下收抱腰间;右拳变掌向前、向上至头顶上方,掌心向上。目视前方(图5-19)。

(2) Keep moving, right foot strides one step forward, close left fist backward and downward against the waist from overhead. Change right fist into palm and shift it forward, upward, and overhead, supinely. Look straight ahead (Figure 5-19).

图5-19(Figure 5-19)

(3)上动不停,左脚向前上步,上体微右转,随即右脚跟进在左脚内侧,脚尖点地,两腿屈膝半蹲成右丁步;同时,右掌向后、向下变拳与左拳同时向左前屈臂撞出,拳心均向下,右拳面靠近左小臂内侧,两拳与胸同高。目视左拳方向(图 5-20)。

(3) Keep moving, slightly turn right, left foot strides forward, right heel advances to left foot inward, tiptoes touch the floor, bend knees on semi-crouch balance into right T step, at the same time, right palm backward and downward, change fists and bump them out leftward and forward, fist centers downward, right fist face against the left wrist inward, keep fists at chest's level. Look at the left fist (Figure 5-20).

图 5-20(Figure 5-20)

13.马步单鞭

(1)上体右转,右脚向右后一步成马步;同时,两臂屈肘收于胸前,两拳心向内。目视前方(图 5-21)。

13. Horse-riding single whipping

(1) Slightly turn right, right foot strides rightward and backward into the horse-riding stance, at the same time, bend elbows in front of the chest, and fist centers reverse sides against each other in front of the chin (Figure 5-21).

图 5-21(Figure 5-21)

(2)上动不停,两肘分别向左右平击。目视前方(图 5-22)。

(2) Left elbows leftward, rightward and upward respectively (Figure 5-22).

第五章 少林小洪拳 24 式

图 5-22（Figure 5-22）

（3）紧接上动，展臂撑拳向两侧摆击，两拳心向下，臂微屈。目视右拳（图 5-23）。

（3）Spread arms and extend fists, fist centers downward, bend arms slightly. Look at right fist (Figure 5-23).

图 5-23（Figure 5-23）

第二段

Section 2

14. 单飞脚

（1）身体右转上起，重心移向右腿，两拳收抱腰间。目视前方（图 5-24）。

14. Single flying kicking

（1）Throw out right tiptoes, turn right, shift gravity center to right leg, close fists against the waist. Look straight ahead (Figure 5-24).

图 5-24（Figure 5-24）

（2）上动不停，左脚脚面绷平向前、向上踢摆；同时，左拳变掌拍击左脚面。目视左掌（图5-25）。

(2) Left instep stretches and kicks forward and upward, change left fist into palm and pat left instep in front of the chest. Look at left palm (Figure 5-25).

图 5-25（Figure 5-25）

15. 海底捞月

（1）左脚向前落步，左掌变拳收至腰间。目视前方（图5-26）；

15. Pick up the moon from the sea bottom

(1) Left foot falls, change left hand into fist against the waist. Look straight ahead (Figure 5-26).

图 5-26（Figure 5-26）

（2）紧接上动，重心移至左腿，左脚蹬地，右脚随即向前跃步，右腿屈膝站立，左腿屈膝上提，身体右前倾，右拳变虎爪，向下抓按。目视右掌（图5-27）。

(2) Shift gravity center to left leg and kick, right foot strides forward, fall and stand firm on one leg, bend and lift left knee, turn rightward and forward, change right fist into tiger claw, grab and press downward. Look at right palm (Figure 5-27).

图 5-27(Figure 5-27)

16.震脚击手炮

左脚向身体左侧下落一步,右脚随即向左脚处收脚,两腿屈膝向下震脚;同时,右掌变拳,左拳变掌,由两侧相向收于膝前合击,左掌扣击于右拳上。目视右拳(图 5-28)。

16.Stamping and hitting cannon

Right foot jumps, left foot strides leftward, right foot stamps left foot step touch downward, bend knees on semi-crouch balance, at the same time, change right hand into fist, change left fist into palm, conduct combined assault from both sides in front of the knees, right fist face buckles left palm. Look at right fist (Figure 5-28).

图 5-28(Figure 5-28)

17.掏心捶

身体起立右转,右脚向右上一步成右弓步;同时,右拳收抱腰间向前、向上勾拳,拳与胸同高,拳面斜向上,拳心向内;左掌变拳收抱腰间。目视右拳(图 5-29)。

17.Digging and pounding

Stand and turn right, shift right foot rightward into the right bow stance, at the same time, retreat right fist by the waist backward, hook forward and upward, keep fist at chest's level, fist face obliquely upward, bend arms slightly, change left hand into fist against the waist. Look at right fist (Figure 5-29).

图 5-29(Figure 5-29)

18.打虎式

身体右转上起,重心向前移至右腿,左腿屈膝提起;同时,左拳栽拳于左膝上,左臂屈肘外展;右拳向下、向右、向上摆至头右上方,拳心斜向上。目视左前方(图5-30)。

18. Tiger subduing

Turn right, shift gravity center to the right leg and upright, bend and lift left knee, turn left fist leftward, upward, rightward and downward and thrust it on the left knee, bend and outreach left elbow; right fist downward, rightward, upward and swings to the rightward and upward, fist center obliquely upward. Look leftward (Figure 5-30).

图 5-30(Figure 5-30)

19.下栽捶

(1)左脚向前落步,两腿屈膝成弓步;同时,右拳由上向下收抱腰间,左拳随即变掌向前下方摆击,掌心向下。目视左手(图5-31)。

19. Downward planting

(1) Left foot falls forward and leftward, cross legs into the bow stance, at the same time, close right fist downward against the waist, change left fist into palm and swing forward and downward, palm center downward. Look at left hand (Figure 5-31).

图 5-31(Figure 5-31)

(2)上动不停,右拳由腰间向前下冲出,拳心斜向下,左掌上旋,掌心向上,收于右臂上方。目视右拳(图5-32)。

(2) Keep moving, punch right fist forward and downward from the waist, fist center obliquely downward, swing left palm upward, supinely, close it upward and rightward. Look at right fist (Figure 5-32).

图 5-32(Figure 5-32)

20.云顶砸拳

(1)身体右后转,右腿屈膝提起,右臂微屈,拳心朝下向上经前胸至头顶上方,左掌收于腰间,掌心向上。目视前方(图5-33)。

20.Butting and smashing downward

(1)Turn right and back, cross and lift right leg, bend right arm slightly, fist center downward and upward overhead via the front chest, close left palm against the waist, supinely. Look straight ahead (Figure 5-33).

图 5-33(Figure 5-33)

(2)身体继续右转,当转到270°时,右脚下震与左脚并拢,两腿微屈;同时,右拳经脑后云手向体前下砸,左掌在腹前迎托右拳背。目视前方(图5-34)。

(2)Turn right until 270°, right foot stamps and close left foot, bend legs slightly, at the same time, right fist hits downward in front via the back of the head, left palm meets right fist back in front of the abdomen. Look straight ahead (Figure 5-34).

图 5-34(Figure 5-34)

21.旋飞脚

(1)身体左转,左脚向左前方上步;同时,右拳收抱腰间,左掌由下向左、向上插击,左掌与肩同高,掌心向右。目视左掌(图5-35)。

21.Whirling and lying kicking

(1)Turn left, left foot strides one step leftward and cross the leg, at the same time, close right fist against the waist, lift left hand leftward and upward from downward, keep the hand at shoulder's level, palm center rightward. Look at left palm (Figure 5-35).

图 5-35(Figure 5-35)

（2）上动不停,重心至左腿,右腿向前、向上、向左(向里)摆击,左掌在右腿摆击至面前时向右(向外)迎击右脚掌。目视右脚(图 5-36)。

(2) Shift gravity center to left leg, right leg straight and swings forward, upward and leftward, bend the knee, sole buckles inward, left hand swings rightward and meets right sole. Look at right foot (Figure 5-36).

图 5-36(Figure 5-36)

22.冲天炮

身体继续左转 360°,右脚下落与左脚并拢向下震脚,两腿微屈;同时,左掌变拳屈肘向下盖压横于右腹前,拳眼向上,右拳由下从左臂内侧屈肘向上冲拳,拳与颏同高,拳心向内,肘尖置于左拳眼上方。目视右拳(图5-37)。

22.Punching upward

Turn around leftward 360°, right foot falls and close left foot to stamp, bend legs slightly, at the same time, change left hand into fist and bend elbow downward against the right abdomen, eye of fist upward, bend right fist and punch it upward from left arm inward, keep fist at chin's level, fist center inward, elbow tip above left fist eye. Look at right fist (Figure 5-37).

图 5-37(Figure 5-37)

23.老虎大张嘴

(1)身体向左后方转动,左腿提膝,小腿随身体左转向后摆踢,力达脚跟;同时,左拳变掌向左、向右、向后反臂搂手,右拳收抱腰间。目视左脚(图5-38)。

23.Tiger mouth-opening

(1)Turn left and back, bend left knee and swing left foreleg backward, at the same time, change left fist into palm and leftward, rightward and backward and pull, close right fist against the waist. Look at left foot (Figure 5-38).

图 5-38(Figure 5-38)

(2)上动不停,身体继续左转,左腿提膝,小腿内扣,左掌变拳收抱腰间。目视前方(图5-39)。

(2)Keep moving, turn left, lift left knee, buckle foreleg inward, change left palm into fist against waist. Look straight ahead (Figure 5-39).

图 5-39（Figure 5-39）

（3）上动不停,左脚向前落成弓步;同时,右拳变掌经胸前向上架于头前上方;臂微屈,掌心斜向上;左拳变掌向下插击;掌背贴于左膝上,掌心斜向上,力达掌指。目视前方（图 5-40）。

(3) Keep moving, left foot falls forward into the bow stance, at the same time, change right fist into palm and parry overhead, bend arms slightly, palm center obliquely upward, change left fist into palm and stretch downward, palm against left knee, palm center obliquely upward. Look straight ahead (Figure 5-40).

图 5-40（Figure 5-40）

以上 3 个分解动作,要连贯完成。1、2 分解动作突出左腿腿法,故名"蝎子尾"。

The above three movements should be successively completed. The first 2 movements focus on left leg kicking, hence the name.

24.迎面搬掌

（1）上体微左转,左脚尖外撇,右掌由上屈肘下切横于胸前,掌心向里;左掌由下屈肘上掤,横至右小臂外侧,掌心向里。目视右手（图 5-41）。

24.Head-on palming

(1)Slightly turn left, swing left tiptoes outward, swing right palm from upper bended elbow to the front chest, palm center inward, left palm cups from lower bended elbow rightward to forearm outside, palm center inward. Look at right hand (Figure 5-41).

图 5-41(Figure 5-41)

(2)上动不停,右脚向右前上一步成右弓步;同时,右掌背朝前,向前迎击,力达掌指,指尖与鼻同高。左掌收抱腰间,掌心向内。目视右掌(图5-42)。

(2)Right foot rightward and forward into the bow stance, at the same time, right palm forward, stretch arm forward and upward to shoot, fingertips upward at nose's level. Close left palm against the waist, supinely. Look at right palm (Figure 5-42).

图 5-42(Figure 5-42)

25.坐山势

(1)右脚尖内扣,左脚尖外撇,身体向左后转,重心移向左腿并微屈;同时,左掌向上、向左下劈,掌与肩同高。目视左掌(图5-43)。

25. Mountain riding

(1) Right tiptoes buckle inward, left tiptoes throw outward, turn left and back, shift gravity center to left leg and slightly bend, at the same time, left palm chops upward and leftward, keep palm at shoulder's level, small finger downward. Look at left palm (Figure 5-43).

图 5-43 (Figure 5-43)

(2) 上动不停,重心移至左腿,右腿屈膝提起,上体继续左转,右掌向上、向前下劈,掌指与肩同高,臂微屈,力在掌根;左掌变拳收抱腰间。目视右掌(图 5-44)。

(2) Shift gravity center to left leg, bend and lift right leg, slightly turn left, right palm chops upward and forward, palm-finger at shoulder's level, bend arms slightly, shift force to palm roots, change left palm into fist against waist. Look at right palm (Figure 5-44).

图 5-44 (Figure 5-44)

(3) 身体右转,右脚落地下震,左腿屈膝提起;同时,右掌变拳由上向下、向右摆至体侧下方,左拳向左、向上屈臂上架至头顶左上方。目视右拳(图 5-45)。

(3) Turn right, right foot falls and stamps, slightly bend right leg, bend and lift left knee, at the same time, change right palm into fist and swing it

downward and rightward, left fist leftward and upward, bend arm and lift overhead. Look at right fist (Figure 5-45).

图 5-45(Figure 5-45)

(4)上动不停,左脚向左下方落成马步;同时,右拳向上架于头顶前上方;左拳下栽于左膝上,左臂微屈外展;眼随右拳向左摆头。目视左前方发"威"声(图 5-46)。

(4) Left foot falls leftward into the horse-riding stance, swing right fist upward and leftward, parry it right-front overhead, thrust left fist downward until left knee, slightly bend and outreach left arm, swing right fist upward and turn left. Look left and cry "Wei" (Figure 5-46).

图 5-46(Figure 5-46)

26.收势

(1)左脚向右收步,两脚并拢,身体直立;两拳收于腰间成抱拳势。目视前方(图 5-47)。

26.Closing

(1) Close left foot rightward, close feet, stand upright, close fists against the waist into holding fists posture. Look straight ahead (Figure 5-47).

第五章 少林小洪拳24式

图 5-47（Figure 5-47）

（2）两拳变掌，两臂伸直下垂于身体两侧，成立正姿势。目视前方（图 5-48）。

（2）Change fists into palms, arms straight and fall against both sides, stand at attention. Look straight ahead (Figure 5-48).

图 5-48（Figure 5-48）

第六章　少林通背拳
Chapter 6　Shaolin Tongbei Boxing

第一节　套路动作名称
Quarter 1　Routine Name

第一段

Section 1

1. 预备势(Preparation)
2. 金沙飞掌(Flying palm)
3. 打虎靠山(Fighting against tigers)
4. 顶心标拳(Centroid fist)
5. 二郎担山(Shouldering mountains)
6. 双关铁门(Double closing)
7. 闪身炮拳(Ducking with cannon fist)
8. 金童献图(Golden boy presenting figures)
9. 千斤砸拳(Hammering heavily)
10. 左右开弓(Bowing left and right)

第二段

Section 2

11. 鹞子翻山(Kites cross over mountains)
12. 叶下藏花(Hide flowers under leaves)
13. 退步插拳(Retreating and thrusting)
14. 单风贯耳(Horizontal punching)

15. 追风相连（Successive swinging）

16. 顺手牵羊（Picking up in passing）

17. 撩阴重拳（Crotch gabbing with punching fist）

18. 猛虎跳涧（Tiger leaping）

第三段

Section 3

19. 执印翻天（Turning and swinging）

20. 天王托塔（Thrusting and supporting）

21. 观景移山（Mountain removing）

22. 珍珠卷帘（Retreating swinging）

23. 雷公飞天（Flying to the sky）

24. 双风贯耳（Blowing ears bilaterally）

25. 勒马按拳（Empty stance plunging）

26. 舞花起脚（Straight kicking and slapping）

27. 舞花坐山（Squatting and parrying）

28. 收势（Closing form）

第二节　套路动作图解
Quarter 2　Figures of Routine Movements

第一段

Section 1

1. 预备势

（1）两脚并立，两臂自然下垂于身体两侧，挺胸收腹，成立正姿势。目视前方（图6-1）。

1. Preparation

（1）Stand up with feet closed, arms fall naturally, throw out chest and withdraw abdomen, stand at attention. Look straight ahead (Figure 6-1).

图 6-1(Figure 6-1)

(2)两臂屈肘上提,两掌变拳抱于腰间;同时,左脚向左一步,与肩同宽。目视前方(图 6-2)。

(2) Lift arms with bending elbows, change palms into fists to the waist; at the same time, left foot steps leftward the same wide as the shoulders. Look straight ahead (Figure 6-2).

图 6-2(Figure 6-2)

2.金沙飞掌

(1)身体向左转,左拳变掌向身体左侧搂手,掌心向前;同时,左脚向左侧迈一步。目视左前方(图 6-3)。

2.Flying palm

(1) Turn leftward, change left fist into palm to swing to left side, palm center forward; at the same time, left foot steps leftward, tiptoes. Look left forward (Figure 6-3).

图 6-3(Figure 6-3)

(2)上动不停,左掌向左搂手抱于腰间;同时,右拳由腰间向前冲击,拳心向下与肩同高,右脚向前跟进时抬腿向下震脚与左脚并拢。目视前方(图 6-4)。

(2) Keep moving, left palm leftward into fist to the waist; at the same time, punch right fist forward from the waist, fist center downward at the shoulder's level. Lift right foot forward and stamp close to the left foot. Look straight ahead (Figure 6-4).

图 6-4(Figure 6-4)

3.打虎靠山

右脚向后退一步,左脚顺势向后收脚,脚尖点地,身体重心移至右腿,屈膝下蹲成左虚步;同时,右拳向下由体侧向头顶上方摆击架拳,拳心向上;左拳向下置于左膝上,拳心向左外侧。目视前方(图 6-5)。

3.Fighting against tigers

Retreat right foot a step, then withdraw left foot, tiptoes touchdown, shift body center of gravity to the right leg, bend knees on semi-crouch balance into left empty stance; at the same time, swing right fist down-up from the side to the position over head into parrying fist, fist center upward, left fist downward to the left knee, fist center leftward and outside. Look straight ahead (Figure 6-5).

图 6-5(Figure 6-5)

4.顶心标拳

(1)身体重心移至右腿,左腿屈膝上提,脚尖向下;同时,右拳由头顶向胸前下压,拳心向下,左拳收抱腰间。目视右拳(图 6-6)。

4.Centroid fist

(1) Shift gravity center to right leg, lift left leg with bending knee, tiptoes downward. At the same time, press right fist from the head downward to the front of the chest, fist center downward, close left fist to the waist. Look right fist (Figure 6-6).

图 6-6(Figure 6-6)

(2)上动不停,左脚向前下方落步,屈膝前弓;同时,右拳向下收抱腰间,左拳向前冲击,拳心向下,与肩同高。目视前方(图 6-7)。

(2) Keep moving, left foot falls forward, bend knee into bow stance; at the same time, close right fist downward to the waist, punch left fist forward, fist center downward at the shoulder's level. Look straight ahead (Figure 6-7).

图 6-7(Figure 6-7)

5.二郎担山

(1)两脚掌向右碾地,身体向右转180°,成右弓步;同时,左拳收抱腰间。目视右前方(图6-8)。

5.Shouldering mountains

(1) Both soles grind rightward on the floor, turn right 180° into right bow stance; at the same time, close left fist to the waist. Look right forward (Figure 6-8).

图 6-8(Figure 6-8)

(2)上动不停,身体重心移至右腿,右脚向前上方蹬地跳起,左腿随即向上跳步;同时,两臂由腰间向上摆击后收至胸前,拳心向里。目视前方(图6-9)。

(2) Keep moving, shift gravity center to the right leg. Jump with right foot forward, left leg follows at once; at the same time, swing arms upward from the waist then close to the chest, fist center inward. Look straight ahead (Figure 6-9).

图 6-9(Figure 6-9)

(3)上动不停,两脚向前下方落地,身体微左转,屈膝下蹲成马步;同时,两臂向下收置胸前,两拳并拢,拳心向内。目视正前方(图 6-10)。

(3) Keep moving, feet fall forward on the floor, turn left slightly, bent knee and squat into bow stance; at the same time, arms downward to the front of the chest, draw fists close to each other, fist centers inward. Look straight ahead (Figure 6-10).

图 6-10(Figure 6-10)

(4)上动不停,两脚向右碾地,身体右转90°,成右弓步;同时,两拳向两侧冲击,右臂微高于左臂,两拳心向下。目视右拳(图 6-11)。

(4) Keep moving, feet grind rightward on the floor, turn right 90° into right bow stance; at the same time, punch fists sideward, right arm slightly higher than left arm, fist centers downward. Look at right fist (Figure 6-11).

图 6-11(Figure 6-11)

6.双关铁门

两脚向左碾地,身体左转180°,右腿屈膝下蹲;左脚向后收步,脚尖点地成左虚步;同时,两臂向下夹肘,两拳向上摆击,左拳在前,右拳在后,两拳心向内。目视左前方(图6-12)。

6.Double closing

Feet grind leftward on the floor, turn left 180°, bend right knee and squat, withdraw left foot, tiptoes touch the floor into left empty stance; at the same time, arms downward with elbow clipped, swing fists upward, left fist in front and right fist behind, fist centers inward. Look left forward (Figure 6-12).

图 6-12(Figure 6-12)

7.闪身炮拳

(1)左脚向前一步,右脚随即向前上方弹击;同时,左拳收抱腰间,右拳变抢手向下拍击右脚面。目视右脚(图6-13)。

7.Ducking with cannon fist

(1) Left foot steps forward, right foot kicks upward immediately; at the same time, close left fist to the waist, change right fist into grabbing hand to slap against right instep. Look at right foot(Figure 6-13).

图 6-13(Figure 6-13)

(2)右脚落步,身体左转 90°,屈膝下蹲成马步;同时,右掌变拳向体前摆击,拳心向内。目视右拳(图 6-14 和图 6-15)。

(2) Right foot falls on the floor, turn left 90°, bend knees and squat into bow stance; at the same time, change right palm into fist to swing forward, fist center inward. Look at right fist (Figure 6-14 and 6-15).

图 6-14(Figure 6-14)　　　　图 6-15(Figure 6-15)

(3)上动不停,两脚向右碾地,身体向右转 90°成右弓步;同时,右拳向头顶上方摆击架拳,拳心向上;左拳向前冲击,与肩同高,拳心向下。目视前方(图 6-16)。

(3) Keep moving, feet grind rightward on the floor, turn right 90° into right bow stance; at the same time, swing right fist over the head into parrying fists, fist center upward; punch forward with left fist at the shoulder's level, fist center downward. Look straight ahead (Figure 6-16).

图 6-16(Figure 6-16)

8.金童献图

(1)身体左转 90°,重心移至左腿,屈膝下蹲;右脚脚尖点地成虚步;同时,两臂屈肘于体前交叉击掌,左掌在上,右掌在下,两掌心向上。目视右掌(图 6-17 和图 6-18)。

第六章　少林通背拳

8.Golden boy presenting figures

(1)Turn left 90°, shift gravity center to left leg, bend knees and squat; right tiptoes touch the floor into empty stance; at the same time, bend elbows and cross arms in front of the body to clap, left palm above and right palm below, palm centers upward. Look at right palm (Figure 6-17 and 6-18).

图 6-17(Figure 6-17)　　图 6-18(Figure 6-18)

(2)上动不停,左掌外旋向上架于头顶上方,掌心向上;右掌内旋向右下方摆击,掌心向下。目视右掌(图 6-19)。

(2)Keep moving, rotate left palm outward and parry it over the head, supinely; rotate right palm inward to slap down rightward, palm center downward. Look at right palm (Figure 6-19).

图 6-19(Figure 6-19)

9.千斤砸拳

(1)右腿屈膝上提,脚尖向下。目视右掌(图 6-20)。

9.Hammering heavily

(1)Lift right leg with bending knee, tiptoes downward. Look at right palm (Figure 6-20).

图 6-20（Figure 6-20）

（2）上动不停，左脚向上蹬地跳起，身体向右转180°，右腿自然下垂，左腿屈膝，脚尖向下；同时，右掌变拳向左、向上经头顶向下抱至腰间，左掌架在头顶上方。目视前下方（图6-21）。

（2）Keep moving, jump with left foot, turn right 180°, right leg hangs naturally, left leg bended, tiptoes downward; at the same time, change right palm into fist to swing leftward first and then upward over the head, then downward to the waist, parry left palm over the head. Look forward and downward (Figure 6-21).

图 6-21（Figure 6-21）

（3）上动不停，两腿自然下落屈膝成马步；同时，左掌变拳向体前下砸拳，拳心向上。目视左拳（图6-22）。

(3) Keep moving, legs fall naturally into horse riding stance; at the same time, change left palm into fist to hammer downward, fist center upward. Look at left fist (Figure 6-22).

图 6-22（Figure 6-22）

10.左右开弓

(1)两脚向左碾地,身体左转90°成左弓步;同时,左拳收抱腰间,右拳向前冲击,与肩同高,拳心向下。目视左前方(图6-23)。

10.Bowing left and right

(1) Feet grind leftward on the floor, and turn left 90° into left bow stance; at the same time, close left fist back to the waist, punch right fist forward at the level of shoulder, fist center downward. Look left forward (Figure 6-23).

图 6-23(Figure 6-23)

(2)上动不停,两脚向右碾地,身体右转90°,两腿屈膝下蹲成马步;同时,右臂向身体右侧撞肘,肘尖向后,拳心向内,拳眼向上;左拳由腰间向前冲击,拳心向前,拳眼向上。目视左前方(图6-24)。

(2) Keep moving, feet grind rightward on the floor, and turn right 90°, bent knees and squat into horse riding stance; at the same time, right arm bumps right side with elbow, elbow tip backward, fist center inward and fist eye upward. Punch left fist forward from the waist, fist center outward and fist eye upward. Look left forward (Figure 6-24).

图 6-24(Figure 6-24)

第二段

Section 2

11.鹞子翻山

(1)身体右转180°,重心移至左腿,右腿屈膝上提;同时,两拳变掌,向上架于头顶上方,左掌在前,右掌在后。目视两掌(图6-25)。

11. Kites cross over mountains

(1) Turn right 180°, shift gravity center to left leg, raise right leg with bending knee; at the same time, change fists into palms, parry upward over the head, right palm upward and left palm downward, palm centers upward. Look at palms (Figure 6-25).

图 6-25(Figure 6-25)

(2)紧接上动,左脚蹬地向上跳步,右脚落地,右腿屈膝下蹲;左脚下落在右脚前,脚尖点地成左虚步;同时,两掌分别向下、向上划弧收于体前;左掌在前,右掌在后。目视前方(图6-26)。

(2) Keep moving. jump upward with left foot, fall to the ground with right foot, bend right leg and squad, left foot touchdown in front of the right foot, tiptoes touchdown into left empty stance; at the same time, palms moves downward first and then upward separately, stops in front of the body, left palm in front and right palm behind. Look straight ahead (Figure 6-26).

图 6-26(Figure 6-26)

12.叶下藏花

左脚向前上半步成左弓步;同时,左掌向前、向下、向左摆掌收抱腰间;右掌变拳向前下方冲拳,拳心向下。目视右拳(图6-27)。

12.Hide flowers under leaves

Left foot strides half a step forward into left bow stance; at the same time, swing left palm forward first, then downward and at last leftward to the waist; change right palm into fist to punch forward and downward, fist center downward. Look at right fist (Figure 6-27).

图6-27(Figure 6-27)

13.退步插拳

右脚向后一步,左脚向后收半步,脚尖点地,右腿屈膝下蹲成虚步;同时,左拳向前、向下格挡,拳心斜向下;右拳由左臂下方收至腰间。目视左拳(图6-28)。

13.Retreating and thrusting

Retreat right foot a step, left foot half a step, tiptoe touchdown, bend right knee and squat into empty stance; at the same time, swing left fist upward and then downward to parry, fist center obliquely downward; close right fist from under left arm close to the waist. Look at left fist (Figure 6-28).

图6-28(Figure 6-28)

14.单风贯耳

右脚向前上一步成右弓步;同时,右拳向右前上方由外向内横击,拳心向里;左拳变掌,由内向外横击在右手腕处。目视右拳(图6-29)。

14.Horizontal punching

Right foot strides forward a step into left bow stance, at the same time, punch right fist rightward, forward and upward from outside, fist center inward. Change left fist into palm, punching horizontally upward at right wrist. Look at right fist (Figure 6-29).

图6-29(Figure 6-29)

15.追风相连

右拳向身体后方摆臂击拳,左掌变拳向身体前上方摆击,两拳心向下,拳眼相对。目视左前方(图6-30)。

15.Successive swinging

Punch right fist backward horizontally. Change left palm into fist to swing upward and forward, fist centers downward, fist eyes against each other. Look left forward (Figure 6-30).

图6-30(Figure 6-30)

16.顺手牵羊

(1)左拳变掌,掌心向前。目视左前方(图6-31)。

16.Picking up in passing

(1)Change left fist into palm, palm center forward. Look left forward (Figure 6-31).

图 6-31(Figure 6-31)

(2)左掌向下外旋变拳,拳心向上、向左下方收拉,抱至腰间;右拳从身体后侧向前、向下砸压于体前,拳心向上;同时,两脚碾地身体左转,屈膝下蹲成马步。目视右前上方(图 6-32)。

(2)Left palm rotates outward down into fist, fist center upward, drawing back left downward to the waist. Swing right palm from back to hammer forward and downward to the front of the body, fist center upward; at the same time, feet grind on the ground, turn left, bend knees and squat into horse riding stance. Look rightward and upward (Figure 6-32).

图 6-32(Figure 6-32)

17.撩阴重拳

(1)身体右转 90°,身体重心移至右腿,左脚向右上方弹击;同时,左拳变掌向上拍击左脚面,右拳抱于腰间。目视左脚尖(图 6-33)。

17.Crotch gabbing with punching fist

(1) Turn right 90°, shift gravity center to right leg, left foot kicks rightward and upward.; at the same time, change left fist into palm to slap against left instep, close right fist to the waist. Look at left tiptoe (Figure 6-33).

图 6-33(Figure 6-33)

(2)上动不停,左脚下落成提膝势;同时,左掌变拳收抱腰间;右拳从腰间向前、向下压拳,拳心向下。目视右拳(图 6-34)。

(2) Keep moving, and left leg falls into knee-lifting stance; at the same time, change left palm into fist to the waist, press right fist forward and downward from the waist, fist center downward. Look at right fist (Figure 6-34).

图 6-34(Figure 6-34)

(3)紧接上动,左脚向前落地,屈膝前弓成左弓步,左拳由腰间经右臂上方向前冲拳,与肩同高;右拳收抱腰间。目视左拳(图 6-35)。

(3) Keep moving, left foot falls forward, bend knee forward into left bow stance, punch left fist forward from the waist at the level of the shoulder, close right fist back to the waist. Look at left fist (Figure 6-35).

图 6-35(Figure 6-35)

18.猛虎跳涧

(1)右脚向身体上方弹击;同时,右拳变抢手向前拍击右脚脚面;左拳收抱腰间。目视右脚尖(图 6-36)。

18.Tiger leaping

(1)Right foot kicks upward, at the same time, change right fist into grabbing hand to slap against right instep; close left fist to the waist. Look at right tiptoe (Figure 6-36).

图 6-36(Figure 6-36)

(2)紧接上动,左脚蹬地屈膝上提,右腿自然下垂于左脚前,脚尖向下;同时,两臂分别由下向上向身体两侧摆击,两掌与肩同高,掌心向下。目视左前下方(图 6-37)。

(2)Keep moving, jump with bending left knee, right leg hangs naturally in front of the left foot, tiptoe downward; at the same time, swing arms down-up separately to both sides, palms at the level of shoulders, palm centers downward. Look left ahead downward (Figure 6-37).

图 6-37(Figure 6-37)

（3）上动不停,右脚落地屈膝下蹲,左腿下落着地成仆步；同时,两掌由上向下按掌于体前,掌心向下。目视左前上方(图 6-38)。

（3）Keep moving, right foot falls, bend knee and squat, left leg falls into drop stance; at the same time, palms press downward in front of the body, palm centers downward. Look leftward and forward (Figure 6-38).

图 6-38(Figure 6-38)

第三段

Section 3

19.执印翻天

身体上起,左腿屈膝前弓；同时,两掌变拳向左上方摆击,左拳拳心向外,拳眼向下,与肩同高；右拳拳心向外,拳眼向上,在左臂下侧。目视左拳(图 6-39)。

19.Turning and swinging

The upper body rises, bend left leg forward into bow stance; at the same time, change palms into fists to swing left upward, left fist center outward, fist eye downward at the level of shoulders; right fist center outward, fist eye upward under the left arm. Look at left fist (Figure 6-39).

图 6-39(Figure 6-39)

20.天王托塔

右脚向左脚后插步;同时,左拳向下经腹前屈肘向左前上方变抢手插击。掌心向上,指尖向前;右拳变掌向上托在左臂腋下,掌心向上。目视左掌(图 6-40)。

20.Thrusting and supporting

Insert right foot behind left foot; at the same time, change left fist into grabbing hand, moving downward via the front of abdomen to thrust left upward, palm center upward, finger tips left forward; change right fist into palm to support upward at the left armpit, palm center upward. Look at left palm (Figure 6-40).

图 6-40(Figure 6-40)

21.观景移山

(1)左脚向左前上一步,屈膝前弓成弓步;同时,右掌由左腋下向身体左下方45°斜插掌。目视右掌(图 6-41)。

21.Mountain removing

(1)Left foot strides a step left forward, bend knee into bow stance; at the same time, thrust right palm obliquely downward from left armpit to 45° left downward. Look at right palm (Figure 6-41).

图 6-41(Figure 6-41)

（2）上动不停，右掌变拳向上架于头顶上方，拳心斜向上；同时，左掌变拳屈肘收至胸前，拳心向下，再向左前方冲出，与肩同高，拳心向下。目视左拳(图 6-42)。

(2) Keep moving, change right palm into fist to parry upward overhead, fist center obliquely upward; at the same time, change left palm into fist close to the front of the chest with bending elbow, fist center downward, and then punching left forward at the level of shoulders. Look at left fist (Figure 6-42).

图 6-42(Figure 6-42)

22.珍珠卷帘

（1）左腿后退一步，右腿屈膝前弓；同时，两拳变掌向下外旋用掌背拍击左腿，向身体两侧摆掌；掌心向前。目视前方(图 6-43)。

22. Retreating swinging

(1) Retreat left leg a step, bend right knee into bow stance; at the same time, change fists into palms to slap at the back of left leg, then swing

sideward, palm center downward. Look straight ahead (Figure 6-43).

图 6-43(Figure 6-43)

(2)上动不停,右脚向后收拉半步,脚尖点地;身体重心移至左腿,屈膝下蹲成右虚步;同时,两臂向体前摆掌,右掌在前,掌心向左外侧,左掌置于右掌腕关节处,掌心向右外侧,掌尖与鼻子同高。目视右掌(图 6-44)。

(2) Keep moving, retreat right foot half a step, tiptoe touchdown, shift gravity center to left leg, bend knee and squat into right empty stance; at the same time, swing arms to the front of the body, right palm in front, palm center leftward outside, put left palm at the right wrist, palm center rightward outside at the level of nose. Look at right palm (Figure 6-44).

图 6-44(Figure 6-44)

23.雷公飞天

(1)右脚向右前方上半步,屈膝前弓;同时,两掌变拳向身体两侧摆击,拳心向上。目视前方(图 6-45)。

23.Flying to the sky

(1) Right foot strides half a step right forward, bend knee forward into bow stance, at the same time, change palms into fists to swing sideward, fist centers upward. Look straight ahead (Figure 6-45).

图 6-45（Figure 6-45）

（2）上动不停,身体重心向前移至右腿,左腿屈膝向上提起；同时,两臂由体侧向体前上摆击拳,两拳与肩同高,两拳面相对,拳心向下。目视前方（图 6-46）。

（2）Keep moving, change gravity center forward to left leg, lift left leg with bending knee; swing fists from the sides to the front of the body, at the level of shoulders, fist centers downward. Look straight ahead (Figure 6-46).

图 6-46（Figure 6-46）

24.双风贯耳

身体向后微仰,两臂随身体后仰的同时,由两侧向后、向下、向前于腹前两掌心相对击拍；同时,左脚向前下落成左弓步。目视两拳（图 6-47）。

24.Blowing ears bilaterally

Bend backward slightly, simultaneously swing arms from both sides backward, downward and then forward to clap in front of the abdomen; at the same time, left foot falls forward into left bow stance. Look at both fists (Figure

6-47)。

图 6-47（Figure 6-47）

25.勒马按拳

左脚向后撤半步，脚尖点地，身体重心移至右腿，屈膝下蹲成左虚步；同时，两掌根对拧后右掌变拳抱于腰间，左掌变拳屈肘下栽置于左膝上方，拳心向左外侧。目视前方（图 6-48）。

25.Empty stance plunging

Retreat left foot half a step, tiptoe touchdown, change gravity center to right leg, bend knee and squat into left empty stance; at the same time, change right palm into fist to the waist, change left palm into fist, bend elbow to plunge downward over the left knee, fist center leftward and outside. Look straight ahead (Figure 6-48).

图 6-48（Figure 6-48）

26.舞花起脚

（1）左脚向前上半步，身体重心移至左腿，右脚面绷直向身体正前方弹踢；同时，右拳变掌拍击右脚面；左拳收抱腰间。目视右脚尖（图 6-49）。

26.Straight kicking and slapping

（1）Left foot strides half a step forward, change gravity center to left leg, straighten right instep to kick straight forward; at the same time, change right fist into palm to slap against right instep; draw left fist back to the waist. Look at right tiptoes (Figure 6-49).

图 6-49（Figure 6-49）

（2）上动不停,右脚向下落地,身体左转 90°,身体重心移至右腿;左腿屈膝上提,脚尖向下;同时,左拳变掌向下拍击左脚跟外侧;右掌变拳收抱腰间。目视左掌(图 6-50)。

（2）Keep moving, right foot falls on the ground, turn left 90°, shift gravity center to right leg; raise left leg with bending knee, tiptoes downward; at the same time, change left fist into palm to slap downward on the outside of left heel; change right palm into fist to the waist. Look at left palm (Figure 6-50).

图 6-50（Figure 6-50）

（3）上动不停,身体向左转 90°,右脚蹬地跳起向正前方弹击,左脚自然下垂;同时,右拳变掌向前拍击右脚面;左掌变拳收抱腰间。目视右脚脚尖(图 6-51)。

（3）Keep moving, turn left 90°, jump with right foot to kick forward, left foot drops naturally; at the same time, change right fist into palm to slap forward against right instep; change left palm into fist to the waist. Look at right tiptoes (Figure 6-51).

第六章　少林通背拳

图 6-51（Figure 6-51）

（4）身体左转 90°下落，两脚屈膝下蹲；同时，两臂向身体右侧摆掌。目视右掌（图 6-52）。

（4）Turn left 90° and fall, bend knees and squat; at the same time, arms swing rightward. Look at right palm（Figure 6-52）.

图 6-52（Figure 6-52）

（5）紧接上动，右脚蹬地上起，身体向左上方转体 180°，右脚向左上前方由外向里摆腿，左腿自然下垂；同时，左掌由左向右拍击在右脚脚掌上，右掌变拳向身体右下方摆击。目视右脚掌（图 6-53）。

（5）Keep moving, jump with right foot, turn left 180°, swing right foot outside-in from left to front, left leg drops naturally; at the same time, left palm slaps against left instep from left to right, change right palm into fist to swing right downward. Look at right sole（Figure 6-53）.

图 6-53（Figure 6-53）

157

27.舞花坐山

(1)身体在空中左转180°,右腿屈膝下落,左腿屈膝上提;同时,左掌变拳向下、向上架于头顶,拳心向上;右拳由下向上经腹前向上至头顶后向身体右侧摆拳,拳心向外,拳眼向上。目视右拳(图6-54)。

27.Squatting and parrying

(1)Turn left 180° in the air, right leg falls with bending knee, lift left leg and bend knee; at the same time, change left palm into fist to parry downward first and then upward overhead, fist center upward; swing right palm down-up via the abdomen to the top of the head, and then swing it downward to the right side, fist center outward, fist eye upward. Look at right fist (Figure 6-54).

图 6-54(Figure 6-54)

(2)紧接上动,左脚向左侧下落,两腿屈膝下蹲;同时,右拳向上架于头顶上方,拳心斜向上,左拳向下摆击置于左膝上。目视左前方;同时,发出"威"声(图6-55)。

(2)Continuously, left foot falls leftward, bend legs and squat; at the same time, parry right fist upward overhead, fist center obliquely upward, swing left palm downward onto left knee. Look left forward and make a sound of "wei" at the same time (Figure 6-55).

图 6-55(Figure 6-55)

28.收势

(1)身体上起,左脚向右脚并拢成站立势;同时,右拳向下屈肘;左拳向上屈肘收抱于腰间。目视正前方(图6-56)。

28.Closing form

(1)Stand up, close left foot rightward to stand at attention; at the same time, right fist downward, bend elbow; left fist upward with bending elbow close to the waist. Look straight ahead (Figure 6-56).

图 6-56(Figure 6-56)

(2)两拳变掌自然垂于身体两侧,成立正姿势(图6-57)。

(2)Change fists into palms, arms straight and hang against both sides, stand at attention (Figure 6-57).

图 6-57(Figure 6-57)

第七章　少林朝阳拳

Chapter 7　Shaolin Chaoyang Boxing

第一节　套路动作名称

Quarter 1 Routine Names

第一段

Section 1

1. 预备势(Preparation)
2. 金沙飞掌(Flying Palm)
3. 白蛇吐信(White snake spitting out tongue)
4. 二龙分水(Double snaking)
5. 古树盘根(Ancient tree rooting)
6. 金鸡独立(Standing on one leg)
7. 海底炮(Continuous Cannon)
8. 鲲鹏展翅(Spread wings)
9. 白蛇吐信(White snake spitting out tongue)
10. 二起踩脚(Jumping and slapping)
11. 顶心标拳(Centroid fist)
12. 转身恨鞋(Turning and centroid pounding)
13. 冲天炮(Punching Upward)

第二段

Section 2

14. 急三拳(Critical triple punching)
15. 弓步架打(Bow stance parrying)

16.猛虎跳涧(Tiger Leaping)

17.马步冲拳(Horse riding punching)

18.左双风贯耳(Left blow ears bilaterally)

19.马步冲拳(Horse riding punching)

20.右双风贯耳(Right blow ears bilaterally)

21.猛虎出洞(Tiger pouncing out of its den)

第三段

Section 3

22.浑水摸鱼(Fishing in troubled waters)

23.二龙分水(Double snaking)

24.接手连掌(Closing hands and punching)

25.蝎子勾尾(Back kicking)

26.连三捶(Successive triple hammering)

27.二起踩脚(Jumping and slapping)

28.回头望月(Back leg kicking)

29.左卧枕(Left turning and striking)

30.猛虎出洞(Tiger pouncing out of its den)

31.挤手炮(Hand squeezing cannon)

32.舞花坐山(Waving and parrying)

33.收势(Closing form)

第二节 套路动作图解

Quarter 2　Figures of Routine Movements

第一段

Section 1

1.预备势

(1)两脚并立,两臂自然下垂于身体两侧,挺胸收腹,成立正姿势。目视前方(图7-1)。

1.Preparation

(1) Feet parallel, arms fall naturally against both sides, throw out chest and withdraw abdomen, stand at attention. Look straight ahead(图7-1).

图7-1(Figure 7-1)

(2)两臂屈肘上提,两掌变拳抱于腰间;同时,左脚向左一步,与肩同宽。目视前方(图7-2)。

(2) Bend elbows upward, change palms into fists against the waist, at the same time, left foot strides one step leftward, the same wide as the shoulders. Look straight ahead (Figure 7-2).

图7-2(Figure 7-2)

2.金沙飞掌

(1)右拳变掌,向左内旋,向下切掌,掌心向上,力达掌沿。目视右掌(图7-3)。

2.Flying Palm

(1)Change right fist into palm to rotate left inward and cut downward, palm center leftward, exert strength to palm edge. Look right palm (Figure 7-3).

162

图 7-3（Figure 7-3）

（2）上动不停,右掌外旋,向右侧前方横击掌,掌心向下,力达掌沿,同时向右摆头。目视右掌(图 7-4)。

（2）Keep moving, rotate right palm outward, strike forward to the right side horizontally, palm center downward, exert strength to palm edge; at the same time, turn head right. Look at right palm (Figure 7-4).

图 7-4（Figure 7-4）

3.白蛇吐信

（1）身体右转 90°提右膝,两掌向上架于头顶,掌心向上。目视双掌(图 7-5)。

3.White snake spitting out tongue

（1）Turn right 90°, lift right knee, parry palms upward overhead, supinely. Look at palms (Figure 7-5).

图 7-5（Figure 7-5）

163

（2）上动不停，右腿前落成弓步，两掌向下收至腰间后再向身体前上方插击。目视前方（图7-6）。

(2) Keep moving, right leg falls forward into bow stance, thrust palms downward from the waist to the front upward. Look straight ahead (Figure 7-6).

图7-6(Figure 7-6)

4.二龙分水

右腿向后退一步成左虚步；同时，双掌向身体两侧下方按掌，掌心向下。目视前方（图7-7）。

4.Double snaking

Retreat right leg a step into left empty stance; at the same time, press palms downward on both sides, palm center downward. Look straight ahead (Figure 7-7).

图7-7(Figure 7-7)

5.古树盘根

（1）左脚向前半步成弓步，左掌向前搂掌，掌心向前与肩同高，右掌抱拳收至腰间。目视左掌（图7-8）。

5. Ancient tree rooting

(1) Left foot strides half a step forward into bow stance, push left palm forward at the shoulders' level, palm center forward, change right palm into fist close to the waist. Look at left palm (Figure 7-8).

图 7-8(Figure 7-8)

(2)紧接上动,右脚从左腿后向左前插步,身体下蹲成歇步,左掌外旋抓棍变拳收抱腰间,右拳变掌由腰间向身体右下方切掌,掌心向下。目视右掌(图 7-9 和图 7-10)。

(2) Continuously, insert right foot rightward and forward from the back of left leg into sitting stance, rotate left palm outward into fist close to the waist, change right fist into palm to cut right downward, palm center downward. Look at right palm (Figure 7-9 and 7-10).

图 7-9(Figure 7-9)   图 7-10(Figure 7-10)

6. 金鸡独立

身体右转重心移至左腿,右脚向前一步向下震脚;同时,左腿提膝,右掌变拳由下向后、向上架于头顶,拳心斜向上;左拳由腰间向下栽于左膝上,拳心向左外侧。目视前方(图 7-11)。

6.Standing on one leg

Shift gravity center to left leg, stamp with right foot; at the same time, raise left knee, change right palm into fist to parry overhead, fist eye upward, put left fist on the left knee from the waist, fist center left outward. Look straight ahead (Figure 7-11).

图 7-11(Figure 7-11)

7.海底炮

左脚向下震脚,两腿屈膝下蹲成蹲步;同时,右拳向下,砸击在左拳心内,挺胸塌腰。目视前方(图7-12)。

7.Continuous Cannon

Stamp with left foot into squatting piling; at the same time, pound right fist downward on the left fist center. Look straight ahead (Figure 7-12).

图 7-12(Figure 7-12)

8.鲲鹏展翅

(1)左腿提膝,两臂向上提至胸前,两掌心向下。目视前方(图7-13)。

8.Spread wings

(1)Raise left leg, arms upward to the front of the chest, palm centers downward. Look straight ahead (Figure 7-13).

第七章　少林朝阳拳

图 7-13(Figure 7-13)

（2）上动不停,左脚向前弹踢,两臂向身体两侧摆击,力达掌指,掌心向上。目视前方(图 7-14)。

(2) Continuously, left foot kicks forward, swing arms sideward, deliver force to fingers, plam centers upward. Look straight ahead (Figure 7-14).

图 7-14(Figure 7-14)

（3）紧接上动,右腿随身体右转 180°,两臂向下摆击收于腰间抱拳。目视前方(图 7-15)。

(3) Keep moving, turn right 180°, swing arms downward and fists close to the waist into holding fists. Look straight ahead(Figure 7-15).

图 7-15(Figure 7-15)

167

9.白蛇吐信

左腿下落右腿前弓成弓步,两拳变掌由腰间向体前斜上方插击,掌心向上。目视双掌(图7-16)。

9.White snake spitting out tongue

Left leg falls, bend right leg forward into bow stance, change fists into palms to thrust obliquely upward from the waist, supinely. Look at palms (Figure 7-16).

图7-16(Figure 7-16)

10.二起踩脚

(1)左脚上提,左掌不动,右掌变拳收抱腰间。目视左掌(图7-17)。

10.Jumping and slapping

(1)Raise left foot, change right palm into fist close to the waist. Look at left palm (Figure 7-17).

图7-17(Figure 7-17)

(2)上动不停,右脚蹬地,向上弹击,左腿自然下落,左掌变拳收抱腰间,右拳变掌向前拍击右脚面。目视右掌(图7-18)。

(2) Keep moving, jump with right foot to kick upward, left leg falls naturally, change left palm into fist close to the waist, change right fist into palm to slap against right instep forward. Look at right palm (Figure 7-18).

图 7-18(Figure 7-18)

(3)上动不停,右脚下落于左脚前方,右掌变拳抱于腰间。目视前方(图 7-19)。

(3) Keep moving, right foot fall in front of left foot, change right palm into fist close to the waist. Look straight ahead (Figure 7-19).

图 7-19(Figure 7-19)

11.顶心标拳

右脚向前上半步,左腿向上提膝,左拳变掌由腰间向前、向左搂手置于腰间抱拳;同时,右拳向前冲击,拳心向下。目视右拳(图 7-20)。

11.Centroid fist

Raise left knee forward, change left fist into palm to brush forward and leftward from the waist, change the palm into fist close to the waist; at the same time, punch right fist forward, fist center downward. Look at right fist (Figure 7-20).

图 7-20（Figure 7-20）

12.转身恨鞋

（1）左脚向后落步，身体向左后翻身180°。右手抱置腰间，左拳变掌向上翻掌架于头顶上方。目视左掌（图7-21）。

12.Turning and centroid pounding

（1）Left foot falls forward, turn left backward 180°. Close right hand against the waist, change left fist into palm to parry overhead. Look at left palm (Figure 7-21).

图 7-21（Figure 7-21）

（2）上动不停，右脚向前一步向下震脚于左脚内侧，身体下蹲。左掌变拳向胸前收抱于右腹前，拳心向里。右拳由腰间向上、向下冲击于体前，拳面向下，右臂在外，左臂在内。目视右拳（图7-22）。

（2）Keep moving, right foot stamps forward at the inner side of left foot, squat. Change left palm into fist to pound to the front of the chest, fist center inside. Punch right fist overhead from the waist, and then downward, fist face downward, right arm outside and left arm inside. Look at right fist (Figure 7-22).

第七章 少林朝阳拳

图 7-22(Figure 7-22)

13.冲天炮

（1）身体上起重心移至左腿,提右脚;同时,左拳向胸前摆击,拳心向里,右拳收抱腰间。目视左拳(图 7-23)。

13.Punching Upward

(1) Shift gravity center to left leg, raise the right foot; at the same time, lift left fist, fist center inward, close right fist against the waist. Look at left fist (Figure 7-23).

图 7-23(Figure 7-23)

（2）右脚向下震脚,右拳由腰间向上经左臂内侧向头顶上方冲击,左拳向下栽置右胸前,拳心向里。目视右拳(图 7-24)。

(2) Right foot falls with stamping, punch right fist overhead via the inner side of left arm from the waist, plunge left fist downward to the front of the right side of the chest, fist center inward. Look at right fist (Figure 7-24).

图 7-24(Figure 7-24)

(3)上动不停,右拳冲至头顶上方后迅速向下落至胸前,肘尖和左拳眼相照。目视前方(图 7-25)。

(3) Keep moving, right fist falls swiftly to the front of the chest after punching overhead, elbow tip faces against the right fist eye. Look straight ahead (Figure 7-25).

图 7-25(Figure 7-25)

第二段

Section 2

14.急三拳

(1)左脚向前上一步,两腿屈膝下蹲成半马步,左拳变掌向前搂手。目视左掌(图 7-26)。

14. Critical triple punching

(1) Left foot strides a step forward, bend legs to squat into horse riding stance, change left fist into palm to brush forward. Look at left palm (Figure 7-26).

图 7-26(Figure 7-26)

(2)两脚向左碾地成弓步,左掌向左搂手变拳抱至腰间;同时,右拳向前冲击,拳心向下。目视右拳(图 7-27)。

（2）Feet grind leftward on the ground into bow stance, left palm brushes leftward into fist to the waist; at the same time, punch right fist forward, fist center downward. Look at right fist (Figure 7-27).

图 7-27（Figure 7-27）

（3）上动不停,左拳向前冲击,右拳收抱腰间。目视左拳(图 7-28)。

（3）Keep moving, punch left fist forward, close right fist against the waist. Look at left fist (Figure 7-28).

图 7-28（Figure 7-28）

（4）右拳向前冲击,左拳收抱腰间。

目视右拳(图 7-29)。三冲拳速度要快,连接要紧,力达拳面。

（4）Punch right fist forward, close left fist against the waist. The speed of triple punching should be swift in quick succession, deliver force to palm face. Look at right fist (Figure 7-29).

图 7-29（Figure 7-29）

15.弓步架打

（1）身体右转180°两腿屈膝成仆步,右拳变掌向右前下方切掌,掌心向

173

下,左拳抱置腰间。目视右掌(图7-30)。

15. Bow stance parrying

(1) Turn right 180°, bend legs into drop stance, change right fist into palm to cut downward to right front, palm center downward, close left fist against the waist. Look at right palm (Figure 7-30).

图7-30(Figure 7-30)

(2)身体上起成弓步,右拳向上架于头顶,左拳向前冲击。目视前方(图7-31)。

(2) Stand up into bow stance, punch left fist forward, raise right fist to parry overhead. Look straight ahead (Figure 7-31).

图7-31(Figure 7-31)

16. 猛虎跳涧

(1)右脚上提,身体重心移至左腿;同时,左臂向下屈肘下压收至腹前,右拳向下摆击置于腹前,右臂压在左臂上。目视前下方(图7-32)。

16. Tiger Leaping

(1) Lift right foot, shift gravity center to left leg; at the same time, bend left arm downward to the front of the abdomen, swing right palm downward to the front of the abdomen, press right arm on the left arm. Look downward and forward (Figure 7-32).

第七章　少林朝阳拳

图 7-32（Figure 7-32）

（2）上动不停,左脚蹬地跳起,身体向右转 180°。目视右后方（图7-33）。

(2) Keep moving, jump with left foot, turn right 180°. Look at right backward (Figure 7-33).

图 7-33（Figure 7-33）

（3）右脚落地,左脚随即向左前方击脚,身体下蹲成左仆步,右拳抱置腰间,左掌经胸前向下切击于左脚面上,掌心向下。目视左掌(图 7-34)。

(3) Right foot falls, left foot kicks left forward at once, squat into left drop stance, close right fist against the waist, left palm cuts downward at the left instep vie the front of the chest, palm center downward. Look at left palm (Figure 7-34).

图 7-34（Figure 7-34）

175

17.马步冲拳

上动不停,身体上起,右脚向前上一步,身体左转180°,两腿屈膝下蹲成马步,左掌变拳抱于腰间。右拳由腰间向前冲击,拳眼向上。目视右拳(图7-35)。

17.Horse riding punching

Keep moving, stand up, right foot steps forward, turn left 180°, bend legs and squat into horse riding stance, change left palm into fist to the waist. Punch right fist forward from the waist, fist eye upward. Look at right fist (Figure 7-35).

图7-35(Figure 7-35)

18.左双风贯耳

身体左转45°,右脚向前上步,身体下蹲成右虚步;同时,两拳变掌由两侧向胸前合击。目视右前下方(图7-36)。

18.Left blow ears bilaterally

Turn left 45°, right foot strides a step forward into right empty stance; at the same time, change fists into palms to clap to the front of the chest from both sides. Look right downward (Figure 7-36).

图7-36(Figure 7-36)

第七章 少林朝阳拳

19.马步冲拳

（1）右脚向右前上一步，两腿下蹲成马步，右掌向体前右侧搂手，掌心向前，左掌变拳抱于腰间。目视右掌（图7-37）。

19. Horse riding punching

(1) Right foot strides a step right forward, squat into horse riding stance, right palm brush rightward in the front of the body, palm center forward, change left palm into fist to the waist. Look at right palm (Figure 7-37).

图7-37（Figure 7-37）

（2）上动不停，身体右转180°左脚上前一步，右掌搂手抱拳于腰间，两腿下蹲成马步；左拳向前冲击，拳眼向上。目视左拳（图7-38）。

(2) Keep moving, brush with right palm into fist to the waist, turn right 180°, left footsteps forward, squat into horse riding stance; punch left fist forward, fist center upward. Look at left fist (Figure 7-38).

图7-38（Figure 7-38）

20.右双风贯耳

身体右转45°，左脚向前上步身体下蹲成左虚步；同时，两拳变掌由两侧向胸前合击。目视左前下方（图7-39和图7-40）。

177

20. Right blow ears bilaterally

Turn right 45°, left foot strides a step forward into left empty stance; at the same time, change fists into palms to clap to the front of the chest from both sides. Look at left front downward (Figure 7-39 and 7-40).

图 7-39(Figure 7-39)　　　　图 7-40(Figure 7-40)

21. 猛虎出洞

(1)左脚向前一步,身体左转 180°,身体重心移至左腿,右腿提膝,两掌随身体左转的同时向左前方做搂手变拳抱置腰间。目视右前下方(图 7-41)。

21. Tiger pouncing out of its den

(1) Left foot strides a step forward, turn left 180°, shift gravity center to left leg, raise right knee, brush with palms left forward following the left turning of the body, changing them into fists to the waist. Look right downward (Figure 7-41)

图 7-41(Figure 7-41)

(2)上动不停,右脚向前落地成弓步,两拳由腰间向前上方冲击,两拳心相对。目视右前方(图 7-42)。

(2) Keep moving, right foot falls forward into bow stance, punch fists for-

ward and upward from the waist, fist centers against each other. Look right forward (Figure 7-42).

图 7-42(Figure 7-42)

第三段

Section 3

22.浑水摸鱼

(1)身体左转,两脚碾地,屈膝下蹲成马步;同时,两拳变掌向身体左侧下击,左掌在前,右掌在后,置于左腿前,两掌心向下。目视两掌(图 7-43)。

22.Fishing in troubled waters

(1)Turn left, feet grind on the ground, bend knees and squat into horse riding stance; at the same time, change fists into palms to strike downward to the left side, left palm in front, right palm behind, palms in front of the left leg, palm centers downward. Look at palms (Figure 7-43).

图 7-43(Figure 7-43)

(2)上动不停,右脚向左腿后插步,身体右转 180°成马步。目视左掌(图 7-44)。

(2)Keep moving, insert right foot behind the left leg, turn right 180° into horse riding stance. Look at left palm (Figure 7-44).

图 7-44(Figure 7-44)

(3)上动不停,以右脚脚掌为轴,身体继续右转180°,左步向右前方上步,两腿屈膝下蹲成马步,双手按在体前。目视两掌(图7-45)。

(3) Keep moving. Take right sole as an axis, continue turning right 180°, left foot strides right forward, bend knees and squat into horse riding stance, press hands in front of left leg. Look at palms (Figure 7-45).

图 7-45(Figure 7-45)

23.二龙分水

(1)左脚向后退步,两腿直立站起,双掌同时内旋,掌心向上,两掌背同时拍击大腿内侧。目视双掌(图7-46)。

23. Double snaking

(1) Retreat left foot, stand upright, rotate palms inward at the same time, supinely, palm back claps on the inside of the thigh. Look at palms (Figure 7-46).

第七章　少林朝阳拳

图 7-46（Figure 7-46）

（2）上动不停，左腿向后退一步成弓步，两掌由身体两侧向上架掌置于头顶上方，掌心向上。目视前方（图 7-47）。

（2）Keep moving, retreat left leg into bow stance; swing palms upward via both sides to parry overhead, palm centers upward. Look straight ahead (Figure 7-47).

图 7-47（Figure 7-47）

24.接手连拳

左脚向前上一步，右脚随即跟进向下震脚；同时，左掌变拳向下收抱腰间，右掌变拳收置腰间后再向前冲击，拳心向下。目视右拳（图 7-48）。

24.Closing hands and punching

Left foot strides forward a step, right foot follows to stamp; at the same time, change left palm into fist downward to the waist, change right palm into fist to the waist and then to punch forward, fist center downward. Look at right fist (Figure 7-48).

181

图 7-48（Figure 7-48）

25.蝎子勾尾

（1）身体左转180°,右脚掌碾地;同时,左脚掌向外、向后擦地撩起后提膝,右拳收抱腰间。目视前方(图7-49)。

25.Back kicking

（1）Turn left 180°, right sole grinds on the ground; at the same time, rub left sole against the ground outward and backward, then kick upward and raise knee, close right fist to the waist. Look straight ahead (Figure 7-49).

图 7-49（Figure 7-49）

（2）上动不停,左脚面绷直用力向前弹腿。目视前方(图7-50)。

（2）Keep moving, try to keep left instep straight to kick forward. Look straight ahead (Figure 7-50).

图 7-50（Figure 7-50）

26.连三捶

(1)上动不停,左脚向前落地成左弓步;同时,右拳由腰间向前冲击。目视前方(图7-51)。

26.Successive triple hammering

(1)Keep moving, left foot falls forward on the floor into left bow stance; at the same time, punch right fist forward from the waist. Look straight ahead (Figure 7-51).

图 7-51(Figure 7-51)

(2)左拳由腰间向前冲击,右拳收抱腰间。目视左拳(图7-52)。

(2)Punch left fist forward from the waist, close right fist against the waist. Look at left fist (Figure 7-52).

图 7-52(Figure 7-52)

(3)右拳由腰间向前冲击,左拳收抱腰间,目视右拳(图7-53)。

(3)Punch right fist forward from the waist, close left fist against the waist. Look at right fist (Figure 7-53).

图 7-53（Figure 7-53）

27.二起踩脚

（1）右脚向前一步，身体上起，右拳收抱腰间。目视前方（图 7-54）。

27.Jumping and slapping

（1）Right foot strides a step forward, stand up straight, right tiptoe touchdown, close right fist against the waist. Look straight ahead (Figure 7-54).

图 7-54（Figure 7-54）

（2）上动不停，右脚蹬地向上弹击，右拳由腰间变掌拍击右脚面，左腿自然离地下垂。目视右掌（图 7-55）。

（2）Keep moving, jump with right foot to kick upward, change right fist into palm from the waist to slap against right instep, left leg leaves the floor naturally and hangs. Look at right palm (Figure 7-55).

图 7-55（Figure 7-55）

第七章　少林朝阳拳

28.回头望月

（1）上动不停,左脚落地,右脚随即落地,身体左转90°,两腿屈膝下蹲成弓步,两手交叉收置于胸前,左掌在上,右掌在下,两掌心向上。目视两掌（图7-56）。

28.Back leg kicking

（1）Keep moving. Left foot falls first and right foot follows, turn left 90°, bend legs and squat into bow stance, hands cross in front of the chest, left palm above and right palm below, palm centers upward. Look at palms (Figure 7-56).

图7-56(Figure 7-56)

（2）两脚向右碾地变成弓步,右掌外旋向上架于头顶,掌心向前,左掌内旋向身体左下方按掌,掌心向后。目视左下方(图7-57)。

（2）Feet grind rightward on the ground into bow stance, rotate right palm outward and upward to parry overhead, palm center forward, rotate right palm inward to press downward to the left side of the body, palm center backward. Look left downward (Figure 7-57).

图7-57(Figure 7-57)

29.左卧枕

（1）身体重心移至左腿,右腿向上提膝,右掌变拳向腹前摆击,拳心向里;左掌变拳向右胸前摆击,拳心向里;左臂屈肘在里,右臂在外。目视右前

185

下方(图 7-58)。

29.Left turning and striking

(1)Change gravity center to left leg, lift right knee, change right palm into fist to swing to the front of the abdomen, fist center inward; change left palm into fist to swing to the front of the right chest, fist center inward; bend left arm inside and right one outside. Look at right front downward (Figure 7-58).

图 7-58(Figure 7-58)

(2)上动不停,左脚蹬地跳起,身体右转 180°,右脚落地的同时左腿提膝,右拳由身体左侧向上、向下、向身体右侧摆击,左拳由下向上、向右、向身体左侧摆击。目视右拳(图 7-59)。

(2)Keep moving, jump with left foot, turn right 180°, right foot falls and at the same time raise left knee, swing right fist from the left side upward, downward and then to the right side, swing left palm down-up, rightward, and then to the left side. Look at right fist (Figure 7-59).

图 7-59(Figure 7-59)

(3)上动不停,左脚下落身体下蹲成马步,右拳向上冲击屈臂置于右胸前,拳心向里,左拳向腹前冲击。目视前方(图 7-60 和图 7-61)。

(3)Keep moving, left foot falls and squat into horse riding stance, punch right fist upward, bend arm to the front of the right chest, fist center inward, punch left fist to the front of the abdomen. Look straight ahead (Figure 7-60 and 7-61).

图 7-60(Figure 7-60)

图 7-61(Figure 7-61)

（4）上动不停，双脚向左碾地成左弓步；同时，左拳向左上方冲击置左肩前，拳心向里，右拳向右下方冲击置右腿前，拳心向后。目视右上方（图7-62 和图 7-63）。

(4) Keep moving, feet grind leftward on the ground into left bow stance; at the same time, punch left fist left upward to the front of the left shoulders, fist center inward, punch right fist right downward to the front of the right leg, fist center backward. Look right upward (Figure7-62 and 7-63).

图 7-62(Figure 7-62)

图 7-63(Figure 7-63)

30.猛虎出洞

（1）两脚向右碾地成右弓步，右拳抱于腰间，左拳向左前 45°斜上方冲击。目视左拳（图 7-64）。

30.Tiger pouncing out of its den

(1) Feet grind rightward on the floor into right bow stance, close right fist against the waist, punch left fist leftward and upward 45°. Look at left fist (Figure 7-64).

图 7-64（Figure 7-64）

（2）上动不停，身体重心移至左腿，以左脚掌为轴向左转180°提膝，左拳向下，经腹前向上、向前、向下收至腰间。目视前下方（图7-65）。

(2) Keep moving, shift gravity center to the left leg, take left sole as an axis to turn leftward 180° and lift the knee, swing left fist downward, via the front of the abdomen, upward, forward, and then downward to the waist. Look front downward (Figure 7-65).

图 7-65（Figure 7-65）

（3）上动不停，右脚下落成弓步，双拳由腰间向前斜上方冲击，左拳拳心向下，右拳拳心向上，两拳心相对。目视右前方（图7-66）。

(3) Keep moving, right foot falls into bow stance, punch fists obliquely upward from the waist, left fist center downward and right fist center upward. Look right forward (Figure 7-66).

图 7-66（Figure 7-66）

第七章 少林朝阳拳

31.挤手炮

右脚向后收置左脚内侧,屈膝震脚;同时,右拳向上在腹前迎击左掌,左拳变掌向后、向下、向腹前迎击右拳。目视右拳(图7-67)。

31.Hand squeezing cannon

Right foot stamps to the inner side of the left foot, bend knee and squat; at the same time, right fist resists right palm in front of the abdomen, change left fist into palm to meet right fist in front of the abdomen, squeeze hands before the body. Look at right fist (Figure 7-67).

图7-67(Figure 7-67)

32.舞花坐山

(1)身体左转,左脚向前一步成弓步;同时,左掌收抱腰间,右拳变掌由上向下抡臂劈掌。目视右掌(图7-68)。

32.Waving and parrying

(1)Turn left, left foot strides a step forward into bow stance; at the same time, close left palm against the waist, change right fist into palm, swing arm up-down to cleave with palm. Look at right palm (Figure 7-68).

图7-68(Figure 7-68)

(2)上动不停,右脚向左脚前跳步震脚;同时,左腿提膝,右掌向下、向右划弧置于身体右侧,左掌从腰间向上置于左体侧,掌心向下。目视右掌(图7-69)。

（2）Keep moving, leap with right foot in front of left foot to stamp; at the same time, lift left knee, wave right palm a curve downward and rightward to the right side, left palm moves upward from the waist to the left side, palm center downward. Look at right palm (Figure 7-69).

图 7-69(Figure 7-69)

（3）紧接上动,左脚下落成马步,右掌向头顶架掌,左掌向下摆击置于左膝上;同时,向左前方摆头,发"威"声。目视左前方(图7-70)。

（3）Continuously, left foot falls into horse riding stance, parry right palm overhead, swing left palm downward on the left knee; at the same time, turn head left forward and make a sound of "wei". Look left forward (Figure 7-70).

图 7-70(Figure 7-70)

33. 收势

（1）左脚向右成并步;同时,两拳抱于腰间。目视前方(图7-71)。

33. Closing form

（1）Close left foot to right foot; at the same time, hold fists against the waist. Look straight ahead (Figure 7-71).

第七章 少林朝阳拳

图 7-71（Figure 7-71）

（2）上动不停,两拳同时自然下垂,置于身体两侧。目视前方(图 7-72)。

(2) Keep moving. Fists drop naturally against both sides at the same time. Look straight ahead (Figure 7-72).

图 7-72（Figure 7-72）

第八章　少林阴手棍
Chapter 8　Shaolin Yinshou Stick

第一节　套路动作名称
Quarter 1 Routine Names

第一段
Section 1

1. 预备势（Preparation）

2. 定心棍（Centering stick）

3. 苏秦背铜（In situ striking）

4. 左右挑棍（Left and right stick picking）

5. 右劈山（Right chopping）

6. 金童击蛇（Golden boy hitting snake）

7. 乌龙摆尾（Snake tail wagging）

8. 左右顶天柱（Left and right butting）

9. 青蛇戏膝（Green snake kneeing）

10. 右挡马（Right blocking）

11. 云棍左挡马（Long stick left blocking）

12. 背棍小提鞋（Sitting stance pressing）

13. 剖腹棍（Stick ripping）

14. 张飞拖矛（Spear dragging）

第二段

Section 2

15.回马盖顶(Backward capping)

16.饿虎拦路(Hungry tiger blocking)

17.拨火凤点头(Poking and phoenix nodding)

18.青龙归海(Snaking)

19.仙人指路(Fingering)

20.蛟龙三缠棍(Winding stick)

21.白蛇吐信(Snake winding)

22.劈山势(Chopping)

23.左右扫蹚(Left and right sweeping)

24.滚身劈山(Rolling and chopping)

25.罗王坐山势(Mountain riding)

26.收势(Closing)

第二节　套路动作图解

Quarter 2　Figures of Routine Movements

第一段

Section 1

1.预备势

(1)立正持棍:两脚并拢直立,左臂下垂,左手轻贴腿侧;右手屈臂握棍中段,棍立于身体右前侧。目视前方(图8-1)。

1.Preparation

(1) Stand at attention holding stick: close feet upright, left arm hangs, left hand lightly against leg inward, bend right arm to hold stick center, keep stick rightward. Look straight ahead (Figure 8-1).

图 8-1（Figure 8-1）

（2）童子拜佛：左脚向左跨半步；同时，左手由下向前、向上翘腕，屈臂立掌于胸前，指尖同颏高，随之右肘微外展。目视前方（图 8-2）。

（2）Boy worshipping the Buddha: left foot strides half a step leftward, at the same time, raise left wrist forward and upward, bend arm and raise palm to the chest, keep fingertips at the chin's level, right elbow slightly outreaches. Look straight ahead (Figure 8-2).

图 8-2（Figure 8-2）

2.定心棍

（1）左腿支撑重心，右脚内侧向左踢棍把，使棍把段向左上绕摆（图 8-3）。紧接着，左手向下抓握棍的把段于左胯前，虎口对棍梢，右手握棍于右肩前，使棍左右斜向抱于体前，右腿屈膝提起（图 8-4）。

2.Centering stick7

(1) Left leg supports gravity center, right foot kicks leftward into the left stick kicking form, make it swing leftward and upward (Figure 8-3). Left hand grasps stick handle downward to left hip, the part between the thumb and the forefinger against stick tip, right hand holds stick to the front of right shoulder, hold stick obliquely leftward and rightward, bend and lift right

knee (Figure 8-4).

图 8-3(Figure 8-3)　　　图 8-4(Figure 8-4)

（2）上动不停,棍梢向下、向前、向上绕至于左侧,在棍绕转过程中,换右手握棍,虎口对棍把,两臂交叉于胸前抱棍。身体微左转;同时,右脚向右落地,膝微屈,重心移向右腿(图 8-5)。

（2）Keep moving, swing stick tip downward, forward, upward and leftward, at the same time, right hand holds stick, the part between the thumb and the forefinger against stick handle, cross arms to hold stick to the front chest. Turn left slightly, at the same time, right foot falls rightward, bend knee slightly, shift gravity center to right leg (Figure 8-5).

图 8-5(Figure 8-5)

（3）上动稍停,接着右腿伸直,左腿屈膝提起;同时,右肘后撤,使棍横抱于胸前,左臂屈肘,左手握拳栽于左膝上,拳眼向内。目视左前方(图 8-6)。

（3）Pause, right leg straight, bend and lift left knee, at the same time, retreat right elbow, bend left elbow, left fist against left knee, left hand fists carried on left knee, fist eye inward. Look leftward and forward (Figure 8-6).

图 8-6(Figure 8-6)

3.苏秦背铜

左脚向左前落步,左手变掌向下压棍使棍梢向下绕环两周后,于身后成背棍;与此同时,左脚蹬地跳起,右脚向前跨步落地,屈膝微蹲,左腿屈膝提起,上体微右转,左掌收至右腋前,稍停。接着左脚向左上成左弓步,随之左掌向左推出成立掌,指尖与鼻同高。眼随手视(图8-7~图8-9)。

3.In situ striking

Left foot falls leftward, change left hand into palm and make it press stick and make stick tip wind 2 circles downward into back stick, at the same time, left foot jumps, right foot strides forward, bend knees and slightly squat, bend and lift left knee, turn right slightly, close left palm to right armpit, pause. Left foot leftward and upward into the left bow stance, left palm pushes leftward into raised palm, keep fingertips at the nose's level. Look at hands (Figure 8-7 to 8-9).

图 8-7(Figure 8-7) 图 8-8(Figure 8-8)

图 8-9(Figure 8-9)

4.左右挑棍

(1)两腿稍伸起,左脚向前跟进半步,上体微左转;同时,使棍把向下、向前、向上绕于体前,与胸同高,左手在腋下握棍,虎口对棍把。目视棍把方向(图 8-10)。

4.Left and right stick picking

(1) legs slightly stretch, left foot strides half a step forward, turn left slightly, at the same time, make stick wind downward, forward and upward, keep at the chest's level, left hand grasps stick below the armpit, the part between the thumb and the forefinger against the stick handle. Look at the stick handle (Figure 8-10).

图 8-10(Figure 8-10)

(2)上动不停,右腿屈膝向前上提,棍把向上、向后、向下绕至后下方;接着右脚向前落地,身体左转成马步;同时,棍把迅速用力向前上挑,棍把与肩同高。目视棍把方向(图 8-11 和图 8-12)。

(2) Keep moving, bend and lift right knee, swing stick upward, backward and downward, right foot falls forward, turn left into the horse-riding stance, at the same time, swing stick forward vigorously, keep stick at the same shoulder's level. Look at the stick (Figure 8-11 and 8-12).

图 8-11 (Figure 8-11)　　　图 8-12 (Figure 8-12)

以上分解动作要连贯完成,此为"马步右挑棍"动作。

The above movements should be completed successively, namely the "horse-riding stance right stick picking" movements.

(3)接上动,以右脚为轴,向右后转体180°,左脚随转体向左上一步成马步;同时右手握棍,使棍梢向下、向右上挑,成马步左挑棍,棍梢与眉同高。目视前方(图8-13)。

(3) Turn rightward and backward 180° with right foot as the axis, left foot strides one step leftward and upward into the horse-riding stance, at the same time, right hand holds stick, make stick tip downward and rightward into the horse-riding stance left stick picking, keep stick tip at the brow's level. Look straight ahead (Figure 8-13).

图 8-13 (Figure 8-13)

5.右劈山

身体左转,重心移向左腿成左弓步;随之左手滑握梢段,右手滑握棍的中段,使棍把向上、向左以把段为力点向下劈棍,棍把与眉同高,左手握棍于左跨旁。目视棍把方向(图8-14)。

5.Right chopping

Turn left, shift gravity center to left leg into the left bow stance, subsequently left hand grabs stick tip, right hand grabs stick center, chop stick upward and leftward, keep stick at the eyebrow' level, left hand holds stick against left hip. Look at the stick (Figure 8-14).

图 8-14(Figure 8-14)

6. 金童击蛇

(1)两腿伸起,右脚向前上步,右手滑握棍把段,左手换握棍,虎口对棍梢,使棍梢向上、向前、向下绕转于右前下方;同时,左手滑握棍把段,两手交叉握棍于胸前。目视棍梢方向(图 8-15)。

6. Golden boy hitting snake

(1) Legs stretch, right foot strides one step forward, right hand grabs stick handle, left hand grabs stick, the part between the thumb and the forefinger against stick tip, make stick tip upward, forward and downward, at the same time, left hand grabs stick handle, cross hands against the front chest. Look at stick tip (Figure 8-15).

图 8-15(Figure 8-15)

(2)上动不停,左脚向右脚并拢,两腿屈膝半蹲;同时,棍梢继续向下绕至后上方,两手握棍上举;接着两脚蹬地跳起,使身体腾空,两腿后背,挺胸展腹,两手尽量后举。目视前方(图 8-16 和图 8-17)。

199

（2）Keep moving, close left foot to right foot, bend knees on semi-crouch balance, at the same time, stick tip downward, backward and upward, hands grab stick upward, jumps backward, throw out chest, lift hands backward as much as possible. Look straight ahead (Figure 8-16 and 8-17).

图 8-16(Figure 8-16)

图 8-17(Figure 8-17)

（3）上动不停，两脚下落成左仆步；同时，右手滑握棍把处，左手滑压棍把段，使棍向前下摔，棍的梢段触地。目视棍梢方向（图8-18）。

（3）Keep moving, feet falls into the left drop stance, at the same time, right hand grabs stick, left hand presses stick and throw stick forward and downward, stick tip touchdown. Look at stick tip (Figure 8-18).

图 8-18(Figure 8-18)

7.乌龙摆尾

（1）两腿伸起成马步势，两手顺握棍，左手内旋手心向上，右手翘腕，手心向前，使棍梢段向上拦拨，棍的把段横于胸前（图8-19）。

7.Snake tail wagging

（1）Legs stretch into the horse-riding stance, hands grab stick, swing left hand into palm upward, raise right wrist, palm forward, make stick tip upward and against the chest (Figure 8-19).

第八章　少林阴手棍

图 8-19（Figure 8-19）

接着两手持棍，左手内旋，手心向下，右手扣腕，手心向后，使棍梢段向上、向前、向下圈拿，两手握棍使把段横贴于腹部。目视棍梢（图 8-20）。

Hands hold stick, swing left hand inward, palm downward, right hand buckles wrist, palm backward, make stick tip upward, forward and downward, hands grab stick and make it against the abdomen. Look at stick tip (Figure 8-20).

图 8-20（Figure 8-20）

（2）上动不停，重心移向右腿成弓步，身体向右倾；同时，右臂屈肘，右手向上翻腕，手心向上，左手继续内旋扣腕，手心向后，使棍梢段向下、向后外拨，使棍右上、左下斜贴于肋前。目视左方（图 8-21）。

(2) Keep moving, shift gravity center to right leg into the bow stance, lean rightward, at the same time, bend right elbow, right hand upward, palm upward, left hand buckles wrist, palm backward, stick tip downward, backward and outward, make stick rightward and upward, downward and leftward obliquely against front ribs. Look leftward (Figure 8-21).

图 8-21（Figure 8-21）

8.左右顶天柱

(1)左顶天柱:身体右转,重心移向右腿,左腿向前跟半步,两腿微屈,左手滑握棍梢段处;右手握棍向上提起,左手握棍向右前推,使棍梢向下立于体前;接着左脚向前上步成左虚步;同时,两手握棍使棍把向后绕至体前于左脚尖内侧上方,左手在上,右手在下,使棍立举于体前。目视前下方(图8-22和图8-23)。

8.Left and right butting

(1)Left butting: Turn right, shift gravity center to the right leg, left leg strides half a step forward, bend legs slightly, left hand grabs stick tip, right hand lifts stick upward, left hand hold stick and push it rightward and forward, make stick tip stand in front, left foot strides one step forward into the left empty stance, at the same time, hands grab stick and make it leftward and inward, left hand upward, right hand downward, make stick stand in the front. Look forward and downward (Figure 8-22 and 8-23).

图8-22(Figure 8-22)   图8-23(Figure 8-23)

(2)右顶天柱:上动不停,右脚向前上步成右虚步;同时,两手握棍使棍梢向后绕至体前于右脚内侧上方,右手在上,左手在下,使棍立举于体前。目视前下方(图8-24)。

(2)Right butting: Keep moving, right foot strides forward into the empty stance, at the same time, hands grab stick and make stick tip backward to right foot inward, right hand upward, left hand downward, make stick stand in front. Look forward and downward (Figure 8-24).

第八章　少林阴手棍

图 8-24（Figure 8-24）

以上两个分解动作要连贯完成。

The above movements should be successively completed.

9.青蛇戏膝

右手向后、向下压棍于右腰间,使棍梢向前上挑,棍梢与腰同高;同时,右脚脚面绷平,向前、向上弹踢,右脚与左膝同高。目视棍梢(图 8-25)。

9.Green snake kneeing

Right hand backward and downward to press stick against right waist, make stick tip forward and upward, keep stick tip at the waist' level, at the same time, right foot instep stretches tight, kick forward and upward, keep right foot at the left knee's level. Look at stick tip (Figure 8-25).

图 8-25（Figure 8-25）

10.右挡马

(1)右脚向前落地,右腿支撑重心,左腿屈膝提起,上体右转;同时,左手向把段方向滑握,使棍梢向上绕至身体右侧,两手交叉抱棍横于胸前。目视棍梢(图 8-26)。

10.Right blocking

(1)Right foot falls forward, right leg supports gravity center, and bend and

203

lift left knee, turn right, at the same time, left hand grabs stick and make stick tip upward and rightward, cross hands and hold stick in front of the chest. Look at stick tip (Figure 8-26).

图 8-26（Figure 8-26）

（2）上动不停,左脚向左落地,左腿支撑重心,右腿屈膝,身体继续右转,随转体方向左手向下压棍,使棍梢向下、向后、向上绕至头前上方,左手滑握棍的中段,将棍斜立于身体右侧。目视前方（图8-27）。

(2) Keep moving, left foot falls leftward, left leg supports gravity center, bend right knee, turn right, left hand presses stick downward, make stick tip downward, backward and upward, left hand grabs stick center, make stick obliquely rightward. Look straight ahead (Figure 8-27).

图 8-27（Figure 8-27）

（3）上动不停,右脚向前落步,重心在左腿成左弓步;同时,左手换握棍,虎口对棍把,使棍把向后、向上、向前、向下绕至体前,与膝同高,两手交叉握棍,将棍中段挟于腋下。目视棍把（图8-28）。

(3) Keep moving, right foot falls forward, shift gravity center to left leg into the left bow stance, at the same time, left hand grabs stick, the part between the thumb and the forefinger against stick, make stick backward, upward, forward and downward, keep it at the knee's level, cross hands to grab stick, hold stick center under the armpit. Look at stick (Figure 8-28).

第八章　少林阴手棍

图 8-28（Figure 8-28）

（4）上动不停,重心移向右腿,身体右转成右弓步;同时,使棍把向右上拨击,把与眉同高,两手握棍姿势不变。目视棍把方向(图 8-29)。

(4) Keep moving, shift gravity center to right leg, turn right into the bow stance, at the same time, make stick strike rightward, keep at the brow's level, hands grab stick stable. Look at stick (Figure 8-29).

图 8-29（Figure 8-29）

以上分解动作要连贯完成。

The above movements should be successively completed.

11.云棍左挡马

两腿伸起,身体左转,随之两臂上举,棍在头上方,棍把向左平绕一周;接着左手换握,虎口对棍梢,右手向前、向左、向下、向后使棍把段绕至腋下,左手随之向后、向右、向前、向左使棍梢平绕;同时,身体左转,左脚向左后跨半步成左弓步,拨棍使棍把段贴于身体左侧,棍梢与眉同高。目视棍梢方向(图 8-30 和图 8-31)。

11. Long stick left blocking

Legs stretch, turn left, arms upward, stick overhead, stick swings leftward a circle, change left hand into grabbing, the part between the thumb and the forefinger against stick tip, right hand swing stick forward, leftward, downward and backward and under the armpit, left hand swings stick tip backward, rightward, forward and leftward, at the same time, turn left, left foot strides a step left foot strides half a step leftward and backward into the left bow stance, swing stick against the left side, keep stick tip at the brow's level. Look at stick tip (Figure 8-30 and 8-31).

图 8-30(Figure 8-30)

图 8-23(Figure 8-31)

12.背棍小提鞋

(1)两腿伸起,左脚内扣,身体右转,两手握棍,使棍梢向上、向后、向前绕至身体左侧;接着身体继续右转,棍梢随之向上、向后、向下绕至右脚外侧,左手向把段方向滑握,两手在胸前上下交叉握棍;随之左脚向前上步,棍梢向后、向上绕至体前。目视棍梢方向(图 8-32~图 8-34)。

12.Sitting stance pressing

(1)Legs stretch, left foot buckles inward, turn right, hands grab stick, make stick tip upward, backward, forward and leftward, turn right, swing stick tip upward, backward, downward to right foot outward, left hand grabs stick, cross hands in front of the chest and grab stick, left foot strides one step forward, swing stick tip backward and upward. Look at stick tip (Figure 8-32 to 8-34).

图 8-32(Figure 8-32)

图 8-33(Figure 8-33)

第八章　少林阴手棍

图 8-34（Figure 8-34）

（2）上动不停，左手换握棍，虎口对棍把，向下压棍，使棍把向上、向前、向下绕至体前下方，左手至右腋下，手心向上；同时，重心移向左腿微屈膝，右脚抬起；接着左脚蹬地跳起，右脚向前跨步，屈膝下蹲，左脚收至右脚跟内侧，前脚掌触地，重心偏于右腿；同时背棍于身体右后侧，左手向后拇指张开，虎口按于脚跟上。目视后方（图 8-35 和图 8-36）。

（2）Keep moving, left hand grabs stick, the part between the thumb and the forefinger against stick, press stick downward, upward and forward, left hand under right armpit, palm upward, at the same time, shift gravity center to left leg, bend knee slightly, lift right foot, left foot falls and jump, right foot strides forward, bend knees and squat, close left foot to right foot inward, front sole touchdown, shift gravity center to right leg, at the same time, swing stick rightward and backward, left hand backward, open thumb and fingers backward, keep the part between the thumb and the forefinger on heel. Look behind (Figure 8-35 and 8-36).

图 8-35（Figure 8-35）　　图 8-36（Figure 8-36）

（3）右脚伸起支撑重心，上体前倾；同时，左腿由屈到伸，脚尖勾起，以脚跟为力点向后蹬出，左手随蹬腿向后撩起，头左转。目视左脚方向（图 8-37）。

（3）Right foot stretches upward and supports gravity center, lean forward, at the same time, bend and stretch left leg, hook tiptoes upward, kick backward

207

with heel as force point, left hand conducts crotch grabbing with heel kicking, turn left. Look at left foot (Figure 8-37).

图 8-37(Figure 8-37)

13.剖腹棍

左脚向前落步，左手在右腋下握棍梢段，虎口对棍把，右手上抬使棍把上挑；接着右脚向前上步成右弓步，棍把继续向后、向下、向前豁把，把与膝同高，身体微左转，两手握棍将棍斜举身体右侧。目视右下方（图 8-38 和图 8-39）。

13.Stick ripping

Left foot falls forward, left hand grabs stick tip under right armpit, the part between the thumb and the forefinger against stick handle, lift right hand to make stick handle upward, right foot strides one step forward into the bow stance, swing stick handle backward, downward and forward, keep at the knee's level, turn left slightly, hands grab stick obliquely rightward. Look rightward and downward (Figure 8-38 and 8-39).

图 8-38(Figure 8-38)   图 8-39(Figure 8-39)

第八章　少林阴手棍

14.张飞拖矛

身体左转成左弓步；同时，上体左倾，右手握棍，使棍把向后、向上、向前、向下绞把下压，两臂微屈将棍中段斜贴于右肋处。目视右前方（图8-40）。

14.Spear dragging

Turn left into the left bow stance, at the same time, lean leftward, right hand grabs stick, swing stick tip backward, upward, forward and downward, bend arms slightly and make stick center obliquely against the rib. Look rightward and forward (Figure 8-40).

图 8-40(Figure 8-40)

第二段

Section 2

15.回马盖顶

右脚向左上步，右腿支撑重心，左脚向后抬起，然后右脚蹬地跳起，左脚向前跨一大步，左腿支撑重心，右腿屈膝向前提起，身体向左转；同时，棍把随身体左转向下、向右绕至身体右侧，接着以左脚为轴，向左后体转180°，右脚落地成马步；随转体，棍把继续向上抢绕成马步时，棍把段由上向身体右侧劈盖，两臂微屈，左手握棍于腰间，棍把与肩同高。目视棍把方向（图8-41～图8-43）。

15.Backward capping

Right foot strides leftward, right leg supports gravity center, lift left foot backward, right foot falls and jump, left foot strides forward a big step, left leg supports gravity center, bend and lift right knee, turn left, at the same time, Swing stick handle left downward and rightward, turn leftward and backward 180°with left foot as the axis, right foot falls into the horse-riding stance, swing stick upward into the horse-riding stance, swing stick handle rightward, bend arms slightly, left hand holds stick against the waist, keep stick at the shoulder's level. Look at stick (Figure 8-41 to 8-43).

图 8-41(Figure 8-41)　　图 8-42(Figure 8-42)

图 8-43(Figure 8-43)

16.饿虎拦路

（1）右手向把段滑握,右脚向左后方撤一步,重心移向右腿,身体右转成右弓步;随体转,左手向中段滑握,使棍梢段向右上横击,棍梢与眉同高,棍把段紧贴右腰间。目视棍梢(图 8-44)。

16.Hungry tiger blocking

(1) Right hand grabs stick, right foot withdraws one step leftward and backward, shift gravity center to right leg, turn right into the bow stance, left hand grabs the stick center, swing stick tip rightward, keep stick tip at the brow's level, stick handle against right waist. Look at stick tip (Figure 8-44).

第八章　少林阴手棍

图 8-44（Figure 8-44）

（2）上动不停，重心移向左腿，身体左转，左手向棍把段滑握，右手向中段滑握；随体转，左手回拉，右手横推，使棍把段向左上横击，棍把与眉同高，棍梢段紧贴在腰间。目视棍把方向（图 8-45）。

（2）Keep moving, shift gravity center to the left leg, turn left, left hand grabs stick, right hand grabs stick center, left hand pulls back, right hand horizontally pushes, swing stick leftward and upward, keep stick at the brow's level, stick tip against the waist. Look at stick (Figure 8-45).

图 8-45（Figure 8-45）

17.拨火凤点头

（1）左脚内扣，右腿屈膝提起，身体右转；随之左手推右手回拉，使棍把向右、向下、向后拨棍于身体后侧后下方。上体稍右前倾。目视右下方（图 8-46）。此为"拨火势"。

17.Poking and phoenix nodding

（1）Left foot buckles inward, cross and lift right knee, turn right, left hand pushes right hand to pull back, swing stick handle rightward, downward and backward. Lean slightly forward. Look rightward and downward (Figure 8-46). This is the "poking posture".

图 8-46(Figure 8-46)

（2）上动稍停,右脚向右落地成右弓步,右手握棍使棍把向后、向上、向左前以棍把为力点下击,棍把与头同高。目视棍把方向(图 8-47)。此为"凤点头势"。

（2）Pause, right foot right fall rightward into the right bow stance, right hand grabs stick and make it backward, upward, and leftward with stick as force point, keep stick at the head's level. Look at stick (Figure 8-47). This is the "phoenix nodding posture".

图 8-47(Figure 8-47)

18.青龙归海

右手滑握棍把,右腿全蹲左腿伸直下仆,上体左转并微前倾,右手握棍把使棍向下、向左沿地面经左腿内侧穿出,左手换握,虎口对棍梢,向右手滑向把段。目视棍梢(图 8-48)。

18.Snaking

Right hand grabs stick, right leg spring sitting, left leg straight and crouches, turn left and slightly forward, right hand holds stick downward, pierce it out from left leg inward, left hand grabs stick, the part between the thumb and the forefinger against stick tip, slip rightward. Look at stick tip (Figure 8-48).

第八章 少林阴手棍

图 8-48（Figure 8-48）

19.仙人指路

右腿蹬直，重心移向左腿成左弓步，随之两手握棍把向前戳出；接着左脚蹬地屈膝提起，右腿站直支撑重心，身体右转，随之右手握棍向上、向右拉举，使棍中段横架于头上方，左手脱棍变剑指向左伸臂平指，手心向下。目视左方（图 8-49 和图 8-50）。

19.Fingering

Right leg kicks straight, shift gravity center to left leg into the left bow stance, hands grab stick forward, left foot falls, bend and lift left knee, right leg straightens and supports gravity center, turn right, right hand grabs stick upward and rightward, swing stick center overhead, left hand lets go stick and changes into finger pointing leftward, palm downward. Look leftward (Figure 8-49 and 8-50).

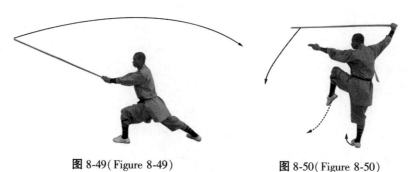

图 8-49（Figure 8-49）　　　　图 8-50（Figure 8-50）

20.蛟龙三缠棍

（1）左脚向左落地，左腿支撑重心，右腿屈膝向上抬起；同时，右臂屈肘，右手握棍下落于右肩前，手心向前，棍梢下落，与左膝同高。左手握棍中段处，手心向上。目视棍梢（图 8-51）。

213

20.Winding stick

(1) Left foot falls leftward, left leg supports gravity center, bend and lift right knee, at the same time, bend right elbow and lower the elbow, right hand grabs stick and swing it to the right shoulder, palm forward, stick tip falls and keep it at the left knee's level. Left hand grabs stick center, palm upward. Look at stick tip (Figure 8-51).

图 8-51(Figure 8-51)

（2）上动不停,左脚蹬地跳起,随之右脚向左跨步落地,腿微屈支撑重心,左腿屈膝脚向后抬起;同时,右手握把向前、向下翻腕压把于腰间,左手向后、向上、向前使棍梢在身体左侧缠绕一小圈,手心翻向下,上体左转稍前倾。目视棍梢(图 8-52)。

(2) Keep moving, left foot falls and jumps, right foot strides and falls leftward, bend leg slightly and supports gravity center, bend left knee and lift left foot backward, at the same time, right hand forward and downward and right wrist against the waist, left hand winds stick backward, upward and forward, make stick swing a small circle, palms downward, turn leftward and slightly forward. Look at stick tip (Figure 8-52).

图 8-52(Figure 8-52)

以上(1)(2)动作为第一个"蛟龙缠棍"。

第八章　少林阴手棍

The above 2 movements structure the first "winding stick".

（3）上动稍停，左脚向左前落地，左腿支撑重心，右腿屈膝向上抬起；同时，右手向上翻腕于右肩旁，手心向前，左手握棍中段，手心翻向下，使棍梢下落与左膝同高，上体微右转。目视棍梢（图 8-53）。

(3) Pause, left foot falls leftward and forward, left leg supports gravity center, bend and lift right knee, at the same time, right hand upward and turns wrist to right shoulder, palm forward, left hand grabs stick center, palm turns downward, stick tip falls and keep at left knee's level, turn right slightly. Look at stick tip (Figure 8-53).

图 8-53（Figure 8-53）

（4）上动不停，左脚蹬地跳起，随之右脚向左跨步落地，腿微屈支撑重心，左腿屈膝脚向后抬起；同时，右手握把向前、向下翻腕压把于腰间，左手向后、向上、向前使棍梢在身体左侧缠绕一小圈，手心翻向下，上体左转稍前倾。目视棍梢（图 8-54）。

(4) Keep moving, left foot falls and jumps, right foot strides leftward and falls, bend leg slightly to support gravity center, bend left knee and lift foot backward, at the same time, right hand forward and downward and turns wrist against the waist, left hand backward, upward and forward, make stick tip swing leftward and a small circle, palm downward, turn left and slightly forward. Look at stick tip (Figure 8-54).

图 8-54（Figure 8-54）

以上(3)(4)动作为第二个"蛟龙缠棍"。

The above 2 movements structure the second "winding stick".

(5)上动稍停,左脚向左前落地,左腿支撑重心,右腿屈膝向上抬起;同时,右手向上翻腕于右肩旁,手心向前,左手握棍中段,手心翻向下,使棍梢下落与左膝同高,上体微右转。目视棍梢(图8-55)。

(5)Pause, left foot falls leftward and forward, left leg supports gravity center, bend and lift right knee, at the same time, right hand upward and turns wrist against the right shoulder, palm forward, left hand grabs stick center, palm downward, stick tip falls and keep at left knee's level, turn right slightly. Look at stick tip (Figure 8-55).

图 8-55(Figure 8-55)

(6)上动不停,左脚向前落步成左弓步;同时,右手握棍把向前伸臂平戳棍,目视棍梢(图8-56)。

(6)Keep moving, left foot falls forward into the left bow stance, at the same time, right hand grabs stick and stretches it forward. Look at stick tip (Figure 8-56).

图 8-56(Figure 8-56)

以上(5)(6)动作为第三个"蛟龙缠棍"。

The above 2 movements structure the third "winding stick".

第八章　少林阴手棍

21.白蛇吐信

左手向右手滑棍把,接着身体微右转,右脚收至左脚内侧,脚尖点地,左腿屈膝全蹲;同时,左手滑握棍梢段屈膝使棍向左平戳;右手滑握棍中段,头右转。目视棍把方向(图8-57和图5-58)。

21.Snake winding

Left hand slips stick to right hand, turn right slightly, close right foot to left foot inward, tiptoes touchdown, bend left knee into spring sitting, at the same time, left hand grabs stick tip, bend knee and swing stick leftward, right hand grabs stick center, turn right. Look at the stick (Figure 8-57 and 8-58).

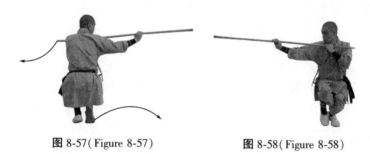

图 8-57(Figure 8-57)　　图 8-58(Figure 8-58)

22.劈山势

两腿伸起,右脚向右跨一步,重心移向右腿,右手滑握棍把处,屈臂上抬,左手滑握棍中段,使棍梢略低;接着左脚向身体右侧上步;同时,向右后转体180°,两腿屈膝半蹲成马步;随转体两手握棍以棍梢段为力点,经头左上方,抡绕下劈至身体左侧,两手平端棍,与腰同高,右手握棍紧贴于腰间。目视棍梢(图8-59和图8-60)。

22.Chopping

Legs stretch, right foot strides one step rightward, shift gravity center to the right leg, right hand grabs stick, bend and lift elbow, left hand grabs stick center, slightly lower stick tip, left foot strides rightward, at the same time, turn rightward and backward 180°, bend knees on semi-crouch balance into the horse-riding stance, turn and hands grab stick tip and make it force point, chop it leftward and upward, keep stick at the waist's level, right hand grabs stick against the waist. Look at stick tip (Figure 8-59 and 8-60).

图 8-59（Figure 8-59）

图 8-60（Figure 8-60）

23.左右扫蹚

（1）接上动,两腿伸起,左脚稍回收,重心移向右腿,左手向右手滑握棍把段,右手脱棍及时向左手前再握棍把段,两手在胸前交叉握棍,使棍把置上体右前倾。目视棍梢（图 8-61）。

23. Left and right sweeping

（1）Keep moving, Legs stretch, close left foot slightly, shift gravity center to right leg, left hand slips stick to right hand, right hand lets go stick and slips stick to left hand, cross hands in front of the chest and grab stick, stick rightward and forward. Look at stick tip（Figure 8-61）.

图 8-61（Figure 8-61）

（2）上动不停,右脚向左前上一步,重心移向右腿;同时,两手握棍向头上平举使棍梢向左绕于后上方,在绕棍时两手滑握棍把段,两臂微屈将棍举于头的右侧后上方。目视左方（图 8-62）。

（2）Keep moving, right foot strides one step forward and leftward, shift gravity center to the right leg, at the same time, hands grab stick overhead, swing stick tip leftward, rightward and upward, at the same time, hands grab stick, bend arms slightly and swing stick rightward and upward. Look leftward

(Figure 8-62).

图 8-62(Figure 8-62)

（3）上动不停，身体左转，重心移向左腿，并屈膝全蹲，右腿伸直向左下仆；随转体仆步的同时，左手滑握棍把以棍梢段为力点，向右、向前、向下、向左擦地扫棍。上体向右前倾，目视棍梢（图 8-63）。

(3) Keep moving, turn left, shift gravity center to left leg, bend knee into spring sitting, right leg straight, downward and leftward and crouches into the drop stance, at the same time, left hand grabs stick with stick tip as the force point, sweep stick rightward, forward, downward and leftward. Lean rightward and forward. Look at stick tip (Figure 8-63).

图 8-63(Figure 8-63)

以上三个动作要连贯完成，此为"左扫棍"。

The above 3 movements should be successively completed, which structure the "left sweeping".

（4）左腿伸起，上体起立，右脚回收，右手向棍把处滑握，左手脱握及时向右手前再握棍把段处，两手在胸前交叉握棍，使棍把段置于上体左前侧。目视棍梢（图 8-64）。

(4) Left leg stretches, stand, close right foot, right hand slips and grabs stick, left hand lets it go and right hand grabs it, cross hands in front of the

chest and grab stick, make stick leftward and forward. Look at stick tip (Figure 8-64).

图 8-64(Figure 8-64)

（5）上动不停，左脚向右前上一步，重心移向左腿；同时，两手握棍向头上方平举，并使棍梢向上、向右绕于后上方。在平绕棍时，两手滑握棍把段处，两臂微屈，将棍举于头的左侧后上方。目视右方（图 8-65）。

(5) Keep moving, left foot strides one step forward and rightward, shift gravity center to left leg, at the same time, hands grab stick overhead, stick tip upward, wind rightward, backward and upward, at the same time, hands slip and grab stick, bend arms slightly, swing stick overhead, leftward, backward and upward. Look rightward (Figure 8-65).

图 8-65(Figure 8-65)

（6）与（3）同，但动作对称，方向相反（图 8-66）。

The items of No.6 and No.3 are the same, symmetric movements, different directions (Figure 8-66).

图 8-66（Figure 8-66）

以上（4）（5）（6）三个动作要连贯完成,此为"右扫棍"。

The last 3 movements should be successively completed, which structure the "right sweeping".

24.滚身劈山

（1）两腿伸起站立,左脚稍回收,重心移向左腿;同时,左手滑握棍梢,右手滑握把段,将棍斜向提于体前,接着身体向左拧转,右手滑握棍中段,使棍梢随体转向下、向右、向后、向上绕至头前上方,左手脱把向右手下再握棍把段,将棍立举于体前(图 8-67 和图 8-68)。

24.Rolling and chopping

（1）Legs stretch standing, close left foot slightly, shift gravity center to left leg, at the same time, left hand slips and grabs stick tip, right hand slips and grabs stick, lift stick obliquely, turn left, right hand grabs stick center, swing stick tip downward, rightward, backward and upward, and overhead, left hand lets it go and right hand grabs stick, lift stick in front (Figure 8-67 and 8-68).

图 8-67（Figure 8-67）

图 8-68（Figure 8-68）

（2）上动不停,身体左转,随之右脚绕过左脚向前,上步扣脚,并将重心移向右腿;同时,左手滑握棍把,右手滑握把段处,使棍梢下落,将棍斜置于身体后侧。目视棍梢(图 8-69)。

(2)Keep moving, turn left, right foot bypasses left foot, strides forward and buckles, shift gravity center to the right leg, at the same time, left hand grabs stick tip and then right hand grabs stick, make stick tip fall, obliquely backward. Look at stick tip (Figure 8-69).

图 8-69(Figure 8-69)

(3)上动不停,身体继续向左后转 270°,左腿屈膝提起,右腿支撑重心,随转体,借助上体的拧劲,两手握棍把段使棍向前、向上猛力向左、向上抡劈,将棍劈至身体左前方,两手握棍于胯旁,棍梢与膝同高。目视棍梢(图 8-70)。

(3)Keep moving, turn leftward 270°, bend and lift left knee, right leg supports gravity center, at the same time, twist, hands grab stick forward, upward and violently chop it leftward and upward and forward, hands grab stick beside hips, keep stick tip at the knee's level. Look at stick tip (Figure 8-70).

图 8-70(Figure 8-70)

以上动作要连贯完成。

第八章　少林阴手棍

The above movements should be successively completed.

25.罗王坐山势

（1）左脚向前落步，重心移向左腿，右手滑握棍中段向上后拉，使棍梢段向上、向右、向后抡棍，上体微右转，将棍斜向横于胸前，接着重心全部移至左腿并微蹲，上体微左转，随之右腿由屈到伸，脚跟擦地向前踢出，脚尖勾起与膝同高；与踢腿同时，棍梢向后、向下、向前、向上挑棍，棍梢同头高，左手握棍于胯前，使棍斜置于身体左侧。目视前方（图8-71和图8-72）。

25. Mountain riding

（1）Left foot falls forward, shift gravity center to left leg, right hand grabs stick center and pull it upward and backward, swing stick tip upward, rightward and backward, turn right slightly, swing stick in front of the chest, shift gravity center to left leg and slightly squat, turn leftward slightly, bend and stretch right leg, heel kicks forward against the floor, hook tiptoes upward and keep at the knee's level, kick and at the same time swing stick tip backward, downward, forward and upward, keep stick tip the head's level, left hand grabs stick in front of the hips, make stick obliquely leftward. Look straight ahead (Figures 8-71 and 8-72).

图8-71（Figure 8-71）　　图8-72（Figure 8-72）

（2）上动不停，身体右转，随体转两手握棍将棍立于身体右前；同时，右腿屈膝，右脚向左脚内侧踏地震脚，左腿屈膝提起，接着左脚向左落成马步，两手握棍将棍斜抱于体前，左手握棍于腹前，右手握棍于右肩前上方。头猛左转;同时,呼出"威"声。目视左侧(图 8-73 和图 8-74)。

(2) Keep moving, turn right, at the same time, hands grab stick and lift it rightward, bend right knee, right foot stamps in left foot inward, bend and lift left knee, left foot strides leftward and falls into the horse-riding stance, hands grab stick obliquely forward, left hand grabs stick against the abdomen, right hand grabs stick above right shoulder. Turn left and at the same time cry "Wei". Look leftward (Figure 8-73 and 8-74).

图 8-73(Figure 8-73)   图 8-74(Figure 8-74)

26. 收势

两腿伸起,左脚向右脚并步直立,左手脱棍将棍立于身体右侧,左手变掌贴立于左大腿侧。目视前方(图 8-75)。

26. Closing

Legs stretch, close left foot to right foot and stand upright, left hand lets go stick and lift it rightward, change left hand into palm against left legs inward. Look straight ahead (Figure 8-75).

图 8-75(Figure 8-75)